THE
HURRICANE
POCKET MANUAL

COMPILED AND INTRODUCED
BY MARTIN ROBSON

OSPREY
PUBLISHING

OSPREY PUBLISHING
Bloomsbury Publishing Plc

PO Box 883, Oxford, OX1 9PL, UK
1385 Broadway, 5th Floor, New York, NY 10018, USA
Email: info@ospreypublishing.com

First published by Conway Publishing in 2016
This edition first published in Great Britain in 2018 by Osprey Publishing

OSPREY is a trademark of Osprey Publishing, a division of Bloomsbury Publishing Plc

Print ISBN: 978-1-4728-3426-3
ePub ISBN: 978-1-4728-3427-0
PDF ISBN: 978-1-4728-3428-7
XML ISBN: 978-1-4728-3425-6

Typeset in Bulmer MT by Deanta Global Publishing Services, Chennai, India
Printed and bound in Great Britain by CPI Group (UK) Ltd., Croydon CR0 4YY

18 19 20 21 22   10 9 8 7 6 5 4 3 2 1

Picture credits

Central Press/Getty Images page 12; Imperial War Museum pages 17, 130; Popperfoto/Getty Images pages
8, 16, 42, 117; William Vanderson/Fox Photos/Getty Images page 14.

Every effort has been made to contact the copyright-holders of the illustrations reproduced in this book.
If any errors or omissions have inadvertently been made, they will be rectified in future editions
provided that written notification is sent to the publishers.

Acknowledgements

My humble thanks go to a number of people who have provided assistance during the writing of this book.
A number of my former colleagues at the Defence Studies Department at the Joint Services Command
and Staff College were keen to see me continue my interest in aviation subjects, in particular Dr David
Hall, Squadron Leader Hedley Myers and Squadron Leader Graham O'Connor. The staff of the JSCSC
library provided much assistance during a research trip in the summer of 2015. The staff of The National
Archives, Kew, have again provided excellent service in handling persistent queries and orders of large
boxes of Air Ministry files. I must also thank Melanie Thomas and Dave Bostock for helping me out
during my Research trip to Kew. My former publisher John Lee must be applauded for the shared vision
to get this pocket book series off the ground. At Bloomsbury Lisa Thomas has displayed much patience
and her colleague Penny 'Hurricane' Phillips has proved an enthusiastically excellent editor. As ever,
Charlotte proves to be a highly knowledgeable sounding board, and Harry and Lysander are starting to
understand the allure of anything powered by a Rolls-Royce Merlin engine.

Martin Robson, Ide, November 2016

The Woodland Trust

www.ospreypublishing.com

To find out more about our authors and books visit our website. Here you will find extracts, author
interviews, details of forthcoming events and the option to sign-up for our newsletter.

Contents

Introduction

'The Hurricane was our faithful charger and we felt supremely sure of it and ourselves'

Wing Commander Peter Townsend

'It was the plane that won the Battle of Britain'

Flying Officer Ben Bowring, 111 Squadron

One question remained in my mind during the research and writing of this book. The Hawker Hurricane was loved by the majority of its pilots, and it comprised 63 per cent of Fighter Command during the Battle of Britain in the late summer of 1940 – so why was its contribution to that epic fight with the German Luftwaffe and to the overall British war effort overshadowed by the Supermarine Spitfire? In part the answer lay in the Spitfire's alluringly radical, almost sensual, lines and its performance, especially its speed. Perhaps more important was the perception of the Spitfire in the minds of the general public (in part fostered by the British Government) and in the minds of the enemy. While German pilots were happy to admit to having been shot down by a Spitfire (the 'wonder weapon excuse'), it was almost humiliating to be shot down by a Hurricane, yet this aircraft accounted for 61 per cent of Luftwaffe losses in 1940.

Such perception belittles one of the most successful and, for the late summer of 1940, most important aircraft designs ever to have made it off the drawing board. But it is typical for the history of an aircraft that is riddled with paradoxes. Equipped with a Rolls-Royce Merlin engine and mounting eight .303 Browning machine guns in her sturdy wings, the Hawker Hurricane traced its origins back to the biplanes of the First World War. It was very much a fusion of the old-fashioned and the new, modern age. By the time of the Battle of Britain, although the design had reached its technical limit, Fighter Command could muster 1,715 Hurricanes to combat the German threat. It was by no means a 'gold-plated' solution to the problem of intercepting enemy aircraft, but the Hurricane was good enough and far easier to produce than the Spitfire.

Obtaining precise production figures is notoriously difficult, but a good enough figure is a total of 14,533 Hurricanes produced between

1937 and 1944. Those Hurricanes saw service throughout the war, and the Hurricane story falls neatly into two distinct phases as recounted by former Hawker test pilot Philip G. Lucas. Phase one was the development of the airframe as an interceptor and its performance in that role during operations in France, Norway and the Battle of Britain. The second phase saw the Hurricane superseded as an interceptor but finding a new lease of life in the form of the Mark II, with a Merlin XX engine armed with cannon, rockets and bombs as flying artillery, providing Close Air Support to Allied troops on the ground in North Africa, the Mediterranean and the Far East until the end of the war.

If the Spitfire can be considered a pilot's dream, an aircraft for *flying*, then the wartime service and testimony of its pilots confirm the Hurricane as a superb *fighting* airframe. To understand why, we must trace the development of the Hurricane back to its origins in the mind of her designer Sir Sydney Camm. Camm began his design career working on biplanes during the First World War and by 1925 had worked his way up to become chief designer at Hawker, a post he would hold for forty years, ending his tenure working on the revolutionary Hawker Harrier in 1965. In an era of boffins, Camm fitted the stereotype perfectly. Driven, irascible, idiosyncratic (bizarrely for an aircraft designer he had a marked aversion to using wind tunnels) and at times a nightmare to work for and with, he had the necessary sheer bloody-mindedness to know that he was correct and to take on an Air Ministry and politicians searching for a cohesive and logical airpower strategy. Air theory in the inter-war years focused on the inevitability of the fact that, in Stanley Baldwin's words, 'the bomber will always get through' any air defence. Moreover, the political classes were late to wake up to the threat posed by the Fascist powers rearming and flexing their muscles during the 1930s.

It is in that context that the history of the Hurricane must be assessed. In 1930 the Air Ministry circulated Specification F.7/30 for a single-seater fighter capable of 250mph. Camm responded with a biplane design, the P.V.3, which was rejected. Undaunted, he went in a different direction, submitting a design for a single-seater monoplane development of the Hawker Fury biplane, but in the spring of 1934 that too was rejected. He revised the design again, this time including retractable wheels; they required a new and thicker wing root, which had the effect of providing the design with a strong undercarriage. Propulsion would come from a new engine designed by Rolls-Royce, the PV-12. Test details of this engine, later known more famously as the Merlin, were made available to Camm.

In September 1934 Camm submitted the revised design to the Air Ministry, who were impressed by the potential speed of nearly 300mph. This piqued their interest – especially as they were aware of the problems Supermarine were experiencing with their design to Specifications F.7/30 and F.37/34 (for details see *The Spitfire Pocket Manual*), which would eventually be christened the Spitfire. Hawker would benefit from a growing awareness within the Air Ministry and political elite that Britain was woefully short of fighters, and that the resulting expansion of the RAF would call for aircraft with which to equip squadrons. Camm's design was concurrent with, but not a direct response to, the Air Ministry's Specification F.5/34 which called for an eight-gun day fighter to replace the Hawker Fury. Camm was still designing an airframe to house four .303 Browning machine guns. A meeting on 10 January 1935 between the Air Ministry and Hawker consolidated the two different strands into Camm's design – often referred to as Specification F.36/34 even though the written specification was not issued, as the design was already in circulation. The most important aspect, however, of all this was the ordering and construction of a prototype, K5083.

In July 1935 the Air Ministry issued a contract to Hawker to supply an eight-gun Hurricane. On 6 November 1935, K5083 took to the air with 'George' Bulman, Hawker's Chief Test Pilot, at the controls. After the Hurricane's first flight, Camm climbed on to the K5083 wing desperate to hear what Bulman thought of his creation. 'It's a piece of cake,' Camm recalled Bulman exhorting; 'I could teach even you to fly her in half an hour, Sydney.' There were teething troubles: the Hurricane had a fixed-pitch propeller, which meant it was a little sluggish during take-off – though this was later resolved with the fitting of variable-pitch propellers and then the Rotol constant-speed propeller. There were teething troubles with the Merlin engine itself. Nevertheless, following trials at the AEE at Martlesham Heath, the Air Ministry were keen for the Hurricane to enter production and on 6 February 1936 placed a provisional order for 600. (At the same time, 300 Spitfires were ordered.) The Air Ministry required a number of changes to the original design for the production model and a particular specification, 15/36, was issued on 20 July 1936. A little over a year later, on 8 September 1937, the first production model, L1547, was available for the RAF. Given the urgent need for pilots to gain airtime with the new aircraft, the Hurricane entered

6 March 1938: Hurricanes of 111 Squadron at RAF Northolt, Middlesex.

operational service on 15 December 1937 when 111 Squadron became the first RAF unit to receive it.

Despite the Spitfire's enduring allure, in the last few years before the outbreak of the Second World War it was the Hurricane that was grabbing the headlines, thanks to one particular event which surpassed all expectations. As dusk fell on 10 February 1938, Squadron Leader John Gillan, the Commanding Officer of 111 Squadron, took off from Edinburgh at precisely 17.05. At 17.53 he arrived at RAF Northolt, having covered the 327 miles in just 48 minutes, at an astonishing speed of 408.7mph – shattering the landplane world speed record. Much of the resulting press coverage ignored the fact that Gillan benefited from a gale-force tail wind (though it earned him the moniker 'Downwind Gillan') and instead focused on the fact that the RAF now possessed the world's fastest fighter then in service – not bad for a design that had its origins in a wooden biplane and still retained a stressed-fabric covering (though later aircraft would carry stressed-aluminium-covered wings).

On 1 September 1939 the RAF could muster 16 operational Hurricane squadrons with another one still working up, a total of 280 Hurricanes ready to face the German menace. They would be needed. On the outbreak of war, four Hurricane squadrons were sent to France. The French called for more, but the commander of Fighter Command, Air Chief Marshal Sir Hugh Dowding, was appalled at the prospect of frittering away his precious resources, which he thought should be carefully husbanded for the air defence of Britain. With the Germans inflicting carnage in Poland, the war in the west became known as the 'Phoney War'. Nevertheless, on 30 October one of the Hurricanes of 1 Squadron, flown by Pilot Officer Peter Mould, shot down a reconnaissance Dornier Do 17P, thereby claiming the Hurricane's first 'kill'.

Further north, with the Russian invasion of Finland, 12 Hurricanes were bought by the Finnish government; they arrived too late to see action in this conflict but would be used by the Finns against the Russians in 1941. They were not the only Hurricanes exported. Airframes were also sold to Belgium, Canada, Romania, Yugoslavia and Turkey, and others supplied to the Irish Air Corps and Russia. Even at the end of the war there was an export market for the Hurricane, with aircraft sold to Portugal and Eire.

In the meantime, RAF Hurricanes had been sent to assist with the defence of Norway against German invasion. Eighteen aircraft were embarked on to the Royal Navy's HMS *Glorious* and on 26 May became the first Hurricanes to take off from an aircraft carrier, the pilots landing ashore at Norwegian airfields for further operations. As if this were not enough, during the ill-fated defence they accounted for around 20 German aircraft and provided combat patrols to safeguard the evacuation of British troops; then, remarkably, on 8 June, ten took off for *Glorious*, with all of them making safe landings on the carrier's deck. It was an exceptional feat of flying, tinged with tragedy: a few hours later, those aircraft were at the bottom of the North Sea after the carrier had been sunk by the German ships *Gneisenau* and *Scharnhorst*, with the loss of 1,515 Royal Navy and RAF personnel.

When the German Blitzkrieg against France was unleashed on 10 May 1940 there were six Hurricane squadrons with a total of 96 aircraft committed to the battle and, despite Dowding's concerns, four further squadrons were added to the fight. Against heavy odds the Hurricanes performed well, but with the German advances and collapse of the French army there were calls for even more Hurricanes to be committed to the defence of France. Dowding resisted, pointing out that defending France and Norway had cost him a third of his fighters and around 40 per cent of his pilots. The job was now to evacuate as many men as possible from the British Expeditionary Force collecting around Dunkirk. Despite the feeling on the ground that the RAF had done little during the chaotic few weeks of late May and early June, Hurricanes – most of which were now once again operating from home airfields – flew numerous combat missions to provide cover for the ground troops. With their help 338,000 men were eventually evacuated.

The RAF had borne a heavy cost fighting in France: of the 261 Hurricanes operating from French soil in 1940, only 66 returned in an operational condition, with 75 lost and 120 damaged. Total Hurricane losses for the campaign (including those operating from home airfields) were 386 aircraft. At first glance this might all seem like a futile waste of resources, but there were some important lessons learned. From their first large-scale experience of fighting the Luftwaffe, pilots started to make adjustments to their aircraft, as recalled by Paul Richey, who flew with 111 Squadron. These improvements included the fitting of rear-view mirrors to cockpits and the harmonisation of gunsights at 250 yards – blatantly going against RAF tactical doctrine, which had envisaged gunnery effectiveness at 400–600 yards. The lesson learned by those pilots who made it back was to get very close to the enemy before opening fire. Even here, the Hurricane's eight .303 Brownings were found to be sometimes wanting in penetrative power. Further changes included the provision of armour plating behind the pilot's seat and the change in underside colour scheme from part black/white to duck-egg blue, making the aircraft far harder to spot from the ground.

During the Battle of Britain the Spitfire certainly held the advantage in both climb and speed, essential in enabling Fighter Command, using radar, to place its valuable resources into position to intercept specific threats as they materialised. In that sense the Spitfire was the interceptor *par excellence*. But the Hurricane had a number of crucial advantages. Given the production problems experienced by Supermarine, when France fell and Germany threatened to unleash Operation Sea Lion, the invasion of Britain, it was the Hurricane that formed the operational and tactical backbone of Fighter Command. On 10 July 1940, Fighter Command could muster 320 serviceable Spitfires and 582 serviceable Hurricanes, with 19 squadrons equipped with the former and 27 with the latter. The main brunt of the German air offensive fell on Air Vice-Marshal Keith Park's 11 Group covering London and the south-east of England. In August 1940 Park had at his disposal 11 Hurricane squadrons compared with six of Spitfires, but with a high attrition rate for the Spitfires, increased production of the Hurricane and its ease of repair, the proportion of the latter had increased. By 1 September 11 Group was operating 13 Hurricane squadrons (including one Canadian) and only five Spitfire squadrons.

The Hurricane was manoeuvrable, with a turning circle of 800 feet as opposed to a Spitfire's 880, and as part of the design process it possessed a thicker wing root which made it more generally robust. This robustness was specifically important with regard to the undercarriage – crucial when most of the airfields it operated out of were grassy strips. Moreover, German rounds often passed right through the early Hurricane's fabric wings rather than exploding. Ben Bowring, a pilot with 111 Squadron, loved the Hurricane: '…as a general-purpose aircraft the Hurricane would beat the pants off the Spitfire… It could take a tremendous number of bullets, because it was made of wood and fabric. It would keep flying almost after it was destroyed.' James 'Ginger' Lacey of 501 Squadron, who had several Hurricanes shot out from under him, noted in a typically laconic tone, 'I'd rather fly in a Spitfire but fight in a Hurricane – because the Hurricane was made of non-essential parts. I had them all shot off at one time or another, and it still flew just as well without them.'

It is no wonder the Hurricane was popular and its pilots loyal to the design. Peter Townsend, who was the squadron leader of 85 Squadron in August 1940, later wrote, 'It was the Hurricane, really, which gave us such immense confidence, with its mighty engine, its powerful battery of eight guns and its feel of swift, robust strength and the ability to outdo our enemies.' Pilots loved the stability the thick wing gave when they were opening fire; 'The aeroplane remained rock steady when you fired,' recalled Douglas Bader. That gave not only greater accuracy but also confidence to the pilot. In August 1940 the pilots of 87 Squadron found out that they were to have their Hurricanes replaced by Spitfire Mark IIs. They complained and kept their Hurricanes. Park himself flew a personalised Hurricane from airfield to airfield during 1940. Pilot confidence in the Hurricane was borne out by the test of conflict against the – thereto undefeated – Luftwaffe in 1940.

Between July and September 1940 the Hurricane was the backbone of Fighter Command, accounting for 61 per cent of Luftwaffe losses. The implementation of tactical and technical changes based on the experience of fighting over France had begun to reap rewards. On 13 August Flight Lieutenant Roddick Smith of 151 Squadron flew the only Hurricane so far to have been equipped with two under-wing 20mm cannon when he came upon a large enemy formation. 'I ordered the attack,' he recalled:

> Telling my pilots (who I hoped were all there, although one section was not visible in my mirror, and my No. 3 could not keep up) to dive through the enemy formation and on into the clouds, as I assumed the rear formation were Messerschmitt 110s and three-quarters of my pilots were new. I opened fire with my cannon at about 300 yards, firing into the general mass as the enemy were in exceptionally close formation. One immediately burst into flames and another started smoking when my windscreen front panel was completely shattered by enemy fire, and I broke away downwards and returned to North Weald.

Smith had, in fact, attacked a formation of Dornier Do 17s, but the increased firepower of the Hurricane and the tactical lessons from France were obvious.

14 September 1940: Hurricane fighter planes taking off from Gravesend, after being refuelled and rearmed, during the Battle of Britain.

Given the nature of the aerial combat in the Battle of Britain, aircraft on the ground were not only vulnerable to enemy attack but also of little use in meeting the bombing attacks of the Luftwaffe. Rearming and refuelling aircraft were crucial tasks of the ground crew, and here the turnaround time for the Hurricane was superior to that for the Spitfire. For the Hurricane, rearming and refuelling involved removing just one wing panel per gun and one for the fuel tanks. To rearm the Spitfire involved taking off 16 panels, eight of which were under the wing. Not only was the Hurricane easier to service, maintain and rearm; it was also easier to repair: during the entire war 4,000 damaged Hurricanes were repaired to bring them back to operational level. Last, and certainly not least, given the high attrition rate for pilots during 1940, new pilots found the Hurricane far easier to fly than the more demanding Spitfire.

At the start of the war, Fighter Command tactical doctrine was committed to the Vic formation of three planes. Encounters with the Luftwaffe over France led to the eventual adoption of their finger-four formation, which provided greater tactical flexibility. A further tactical development from 1940 was Douglas Bader's Duxford Big Wing concept. Bader wanted his squadrons to form up into a cohesive large formation before entering battle and achieving a decisive effect – which ran contrary to Park's doctrine of using individual squadrons for a rolling attack on enemy large formations to keep them under constant pressure. While Bader had his supporters, the main problem with his concept was the time taken to form up. On Saturday 7 September, for example, as the Luftwaffe switched from attacking airfields to targeting London in mass raids, Fighter Command scrambled all available resources. As aircraft turned, dived, climbed and fought, Bader's Duxford Wing had still not formed up properly when it entered the battle; it was savaged by Bf109s, which shot down 15 of its Hurricanes. As Roddick Smith had found out, big formations made big targets.

By October 1940 the Luftwaffe had had enough; it had, for the first time, more than met its match in the Hurricanes and Spitfires of Fighter Command. By this time, many of the pre-war pilots had been killed, as indeed were many of 'The Few', comprising British, Polish, Americans, Canadians, Czechs and South Africans, who had fought for the defence of Britain. By the time the battle was won, one of the leading Battle of Britain aces, a flight sergeant with 17 kills to his name, was also dead. His name was Josef František, he was

Czech, from No. 303 (Polish) Squadron, and he flew a Hurricane in defence of Britain.

In winning the air battle against the Luftwaffe the Hurricanes and pilots of Fighter Command had certainly cemented their place in history. Even during this fight, the Hurricane's role as an interceptor was already under threat from more technically advanced aircraft such as the Spitfire. But the Hurricane's usefulness did not end. Taking off from and landing on HMS *Glorious* in 1940 had already displayed some advantage in the aircraft's taking to the sea. Now the Hurricane was to be embarked upon catapult aircraft merchantmen, known as CAM ships, to provide air cover to the valuable convoys that Britain needed to continue her fight against Nazi Germany. Upon sighting or attack from an enemy U-boat or aircraft, the 'Hurricat', as it was known, would be propelled from the ship by means of a rocket-powered catapult, to provide air cover. The aircraft was considered 'expendable' in its convoy-protection duty and was piloted by a volunteer who would either try to make landfall or be rescued on ditching his Hurricane. More promising was the decision in 1940 to convert existing aircraft to Sea Hurricanes to operate off Royal Navy ships with the Fleet Air Arm.

10 December 1940: two Czech pilots watching colleagues
take to the air in their Hurricanes.

Yet the Hurricane could still hold its own as an interceptor, and in the Mediterranean Hurricanes were launched from carriers to land at Malta to provide air defence to that strategically important island. On 13 April 1941 Flying Officer Ishmi Mason was scrambled to intercept enemy aircraft. Coming out of the sun, he dived down onto four Messerschmitts, shooting up one before breaking away from his attack. At that point:

> ...one of the other three got a lucky shot at me and hit my hand and shattered my windscreen. I was now about 15 miles from land, five miles high and helpless, so I had to fight my way back as best I could with this chap firing at me all the time. The instruments smashed up in front of me and the controls went funny, bullets flying through the cockpit. He kept firing from the beam. My right hand was numb. Finally, when I was twisting and turning a few feet off the sea, the motor stopped and the left side started burning. So I landed in the water, foolishly undoing my straps. I broke my nose on the windscreen frame and climbed out before it sank.

Four miles from land, bleeding heavily and with only one good hand to swim with, Mason was lucky to be picked up by a motorboat. Apart from his broken nose, the German bullets had severed an artery in his wrist while another had passed through the flesh of his left elbow. Shrapnel was found in his left leg and skull.

Sea Hurricanes – 885 NAS on HMS *Victorious*.

The Mark II Hawker 'Hurricanes' in flight, c. 1943. The Hawker 'Hurricane', the work of Sydney Camm, was the first monoplane fighter to exceed 300mph, and was first used by Britain's RAF in 1937, becoming at the time of the Battle of Britain the mainstay of Britain's fighter air defence.

By 1942 convoys to Malta were accorded immense strategic priority to allow the build-up of British forces in North Africa for the Battle of El-Alamein. Here, during Operation Pedestal, a convoy of 14 merchantmen was escorted by four carriers with a total of 39 Sea Hurricanes. In total 414 Hurricanes contributed to the defence of Malta: 333 arriving from the deck of a carrier; 62 coming from North Africa; and 19 arriving on merchant ships. Sea Hurricanes also provided air cover during the Allied Torch landings in North Africa during early 1943, but by this time the 800 Sea Hurricanes had largely had their day, with specialist naval aviation aircraft taking their place.

The Hurricane's adaptability once again came to the fore with the Allies moving from a defensive to a more aggressive strategy. The impact would be felt in the Western Desert, where Hurricanes had been deployed in 1941 as conventional interceptors, but already local modifications had been made to turn some airframes into tactical photo-reconnaissance aircraft. At the start of the war, investigations had been made into tropicalising Hurricanes for the punishing desert conditions, and by 1942 the Mark II Hurricane was making a difference, not only providing air defence but in a ground-attack role as

'Hurribombers'. Trials were carried out by the Air Fighting Development Unit at Duxford in 1941, including the use of 20mm Hispano cannon and bombs. At El-Alamein in October 1942 Air Marshal Arthur Tedder, commander of RAF Middle East Command, could field 16 Hurricane squadrons, three of which were designated as ground attack. Typical was an attack on 24 October when the Hurricanes of 80 Squadron provided top cover to the ground-attack Hurricanes of 6 Squadron which claimed 18 enemy tanks. No. 6 Squadron continued to serve in the theatre; by the time it was operating in Italy in 1944 its Hurricanes were armed with three-inch rockets, and by war's end in 1945 it was operating out of Yugoslavia.

Rockets also provided greater hitting power at sea where Hurricane Mark IVs were used to attack enemy shipping. Such attacks were carefully timed to occur between four nights before and four nights after the full moon. The Hurricanes entered a shallow glide at around 230mph and released their rockets 600 yards from the target before violently breaking away to avoid damage from the resulting detonations. Against heavily defended shipping only one attack was made, with aircraft releasing a salvo of four to eight rockets. Against lightly defended shipping, where more than one attack could be made, then each attack released a salvo of two rockets.

Armourers fit rocket-projectiles to Hawker Hurricane Mark IVs of No. 170 Wing in dispersal on an airfield in Burma.

Hurricanes also gave sterling service in the Far East. Stripped down and packed into crates, the aircraft arrived in Singapore on 3 January. Eventually four squadrons were based there but, despite shooting down a number of Japanese aircraft, could not prevent the fall of Singapore on 15 February. The remaining Hurricanes flew to Sumatra. Hurricanes saw further service during the campaigns in Burma where they provided support to the Chindit infiltration operations under the mercurial Orde Wingate. The Chindits, operating behind enemy lines, required supply drops from Douglas Dakotas, and Hurricanes provided the cover to those supply flights. Later, at the epic defence of Imphal, Hurricanes once again provided security to air drops while also maintaining their ground-attack capability; in the first two weeks of April 1944 Hurricanes flew around 6,000 sorties over Burma.

By this time the final Hurricane models were rolling off the production lines, with the last aircraft, PZ865, which carried the name 'The Last of the Many', at the centre of a ceremony in July 1944 to mark the end of Hurricane production. After the ceremony, George Bulman took PZ865 for its test flight: nine years after flying the first Hurricane, K5083, Bulman flew the last. This aircraft was bought back from the Air Ministry by Hawker and took part in a number of post-war air races, as well as starring in the 1969 film *The Battle of Britain*. In 1972 it was handed over to the Battle of Britain Memorial Flight and it can still be seen performing in the skies over Britain. Since 2012 it has carried the colour scheme and markings of 34 Squadron's Hurricane Mk IIC HW840, 'EG-S', which was flown by Flight Lieutenant Jimmy Whalen DFC during operations above Burma in 1944. On 18 April 1944 Whalen, an ace with six confirmed enemy 'kills' to his name, 'bought it' in the skies over Burma.

Given the affection in which the Hurricane was held by its pilots, perhaps the last word is best left to someone who really knew the aircraft inside out. Roland 'Bee' Beaumont saw service flying Hurricanes with 87 Squadron in France and during the Battle of Britain, then in late 1941 was sent to Hawker as a test pilot. He clocked up around 700 hours flying Hurricanes and flew 400 production test flights. Asked to summarise the key attributes of the aircraft, he noted its structural integrity and manoeuvrability. Of his experiences in 1940 he recalled, 'The Hurricane could outmanoeuvre any aeroplane it met at that time,' including the

Me109, and was the most accurate and stable gun platform of its day. Beaumont continued:

> We believed at that time, and I still believe today, that for the fighter combat up to 23,000ft, which was where all the air battles of that time were being fought, the Hurricane was the finest fighter of its day.

88mm gun barrel of a Tiger Mk VI tank penetrated by a Hurricane-fired rocket projectile.

Significant Hurricane Variants

Name	Engine	Armament
Mark I	Merlin III	8 × .303 in wings
Mark IIA	Merlin XX	8 × .303 in wings
Mark IIB	Merlin XX	12 × .303 in wings
Mark IIC	Merlin XX	4 × 20mm cannon in wings
Mark IV	Merlin XX	2 × .303 in wings, 2 × 40mm cannon underslung wings
Mark IV	Merlin XX	2 × .303 in wings, 8 × 60lb RPs underwings
Mark V ('S' guns)	Merlin 27	2 × .303 in wings, 2 × 40mm cannon underslung wings
Mark V (RP)	Merlin 27	2 × .303 in wings, 8 × 60lb RPs underwings
Sea Hurricane	Merlin III	8 × .303 in wings

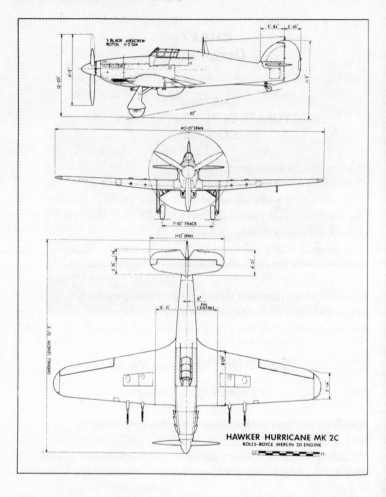

HAWKER HURRICANE MK 2C
ROLLS-ROYCE MERLIN 20 ENGINE

CHAPTER I
Design and trials

AIR MINISTRY.
DIRECTORATE OF TECHNICAL DEVELOPMENT.
CONFIDENTIAL.

This document is the property of H.M. Government.

    This document is intended for the use of the recipient only and may be used only in connection with work carried out for or on behalf of H.M. Government. The unauthorized retention or destruction of this document, or the disclosure of its contents to any unauthorized person, is forbidden.

    Attention is hereby called to the fact that failure to comply with any one of the above instructions is an infraction of the Official Secrets Act.

Note: Any person other than the authorized holder upon obtaining possession of this document by finding or otherwise should forward it together with his name and address in a closed envelope to THE SECRETARY, AIR MINISTRY, KINGSWAY, LONDON, W.C.2. Letter postage need not be prepaid; other postage will be refunded.

Specification No. F.5/34.
Single-seat Fighter.
Specification of Particular Requirements to accompany the Contract Agreement.

———————————————

    This Specification is to be regarded for contract purposes as forming part of the Contract Agreement and being subject to the same general conditions.

Approved by: (Signed) J. S. Buchanan,
Deputy Director,
For Director of Technical Development.
Date: 16th November, 1934.

1. General.

(a) The speed excess of a modern fighter over that of a contemporary bomber has so reduced the chance of repeated attacks by the same fighter(s) that it becomes essential to obtain decisive results in the short space of time offered for one attack only. This specification is issued, therefore, to govern the production of a day fighter in which speed in overtaking an enemy at 15,000 ft., combined with rapid climb to this height, is of primary importance. The best speed possible must be aimed at for all heights between 5,000 and 15,000 feet. In conjunction with this performance the maximum hitting power must be aimed at, and 8 machine guns are considered advisable.

(b) The component parts of the aircraft are to be suitable as regards size, etc., for conveyance by ordinary rail transport or Royal Air Force M.T. vehicles.

(c) The working drawings of component parts of the aircraft are to accord as fully as possible with the requirements stated in Specification No. 16 (Miscellaneous) so that if (in the event of the aircraft being adopted for use in the Royal Air Force) parts are required to be manufactured in series, each member of a series will be strictly interchangeable with the original part.

(d) Subject only to the proviso at the end of this clause, the aircraft is to be designed, constructed and equipped in strict accordance with the requirements detailed herein and to the satisfaction of the Director of Technical Development (herein after referred to as "the D.T.D."); is to comply with the requirements notified in all relevant Aircraft Design Memoranda (whether cited herein or not) and is to fulfil the requirements of the Director of Aeronautical Inspection as regards materials and workmanship. The D.T.D. will, if he thinks fit, modify or waive any requirement which the tenderer considers there may be real difficulty in meeting or which might entail serious delay in the production of the aircraft; any representations in these respects should accompany the tender.

(e) It shall be understood as regards any specification, Air Publication, Standard Instruction Sheet or Aircraft Design Memorandum cited or referred to herein that the reference is to the current issue thereof.

2. Pilot's Station.

(a) An enclosed cockpit is admissible, it is to be draught-proof and provided with satisfactory ventilating arrangements.

(b) The arrangement of the cockpit shall provide the comfort and freedom of movement necessary to enable the pilot to perform his duties efficiently.

Provision is to be made for warming it with waste heat tapped from the engine exhaust or cooling system.

(c) The pilot's seat and the rudder bar are to be adjustable in flight through a 4-inch range, the former vertically and the latter in the fore-and-aft direction.

(d) The view for searching, fighting and formation flying (whether the aircraft is a leader or otherwise) shall be the best possible. The least important hemisphere is that directly below the pilot. In particular, it is requisite that the pilot, with his harness fastened and the seat at its usual height, shall have a clear view directly ahead through an angle of 10° down from the horizontal.

(e) The construction of the cockpit and the arrangement of the equipment therein shall permit free movement in an emergency that obliges the pilot to take to his parachute. An emergency exit shall be provided, together with foot and/or hand-holds or equivalent aids to easy and rapid egress from the aircraft in the circumstances referred to above or in the event of it crashing or overturning on the ground.

3. Armament.

(a) The aircraft is to be equipped with 8 Browning machine guns, adjustable both laterally and vertically for ranging on a target 200 yards away. Electrical or other non-mechanical arrangements for firing are to be incorporated.

(b) The gun installation arrangements should be such that, whilst the drag attributable to them will be a minimum, each gun may be removed, replaced, or re-loaded with ammunition easily and expeditiously. The guns should all be positioned in the wings and outside the airscrew disc.

(c) Stowage for 300 rounds of small arm ammunition per gun is to be provided.

(d) A reflector sight is to be fitted.

(e) Provision is to be made for disposing of the 300 empty cartridges and links in such a way as to endure that there is no danger of their jamming any mechanism or striking any part of the aircraft.

(f) Provision is to be made so that a camera gun, Type G. 22, may be fitted to the aircraft in accordance with Aircraft Design Memorandum No. 195.

4. Provision of Mock-Up.

(a) In order that the proposed disposition of the pilot, armament, etc., may be properly examined and approved on behalf of the D.T.D. before construction is commenced, the Contractor is required to provide a full-sized and (where essential) accurately dimensioned "mock-up" of the aircraft at his works. This mock-up shall include all parts that are likely to interfere with the view from the cockpit and/or with the fields of fire for the guns, and is to show the disposition of equipment in the cockpit and elsewhere and such details of the engine installation as the arrangements for engine-starting and the position of cocks, pumps etc. The instruments and equipment (whether real or dummy) included in the mock-up are to be of the correct sizes.

(b) The mock-up is to be inclinable at the cruising and alighting attitudes of the aircraft.

(c) The mock-up is not to be dismantled before the final examination of the actual aircraft has taken place. Until then it must be available for examination by the D.T.D. or his authorised representative whenever required.

(d) Instructions regarding the drawings, etc., which the Contractor will be required to supply as a result of the mock-up conference are given in clauses 25 (a) and 25 (b).

5. Materials of Construction.

(a) All parts of the aircraft that contribute to its strength in flight are to be of metal.

(b) Main-plane and other coverings are excluded from the scope of the preceding clause and may be made of fabric.

(c) Wherever possible, the materials used in the construction of the aircraft are to be in accordance with current B. S. specifications or others approved by the D.T.D. A list of the approved specifications showing the latest issue numbers, can be obtained from the D.T.D. (R.T.P.).

(d) If the contractor proposes to use any material for which an approved specification is not extant, he shall –

(i) Give the D.T.D. written notice of his intention and
(ii) Supply such information regarding, and test pieces of, the material in question as are considered by the D.T.D. to be required in order that its properties may be fully determined.

(e) All A.G.S. parts incorporated in the aircraft are to be in accordance with the latest issues of the relevant drawings. The issue numbers of such drawings are not to be quoted on the aircraft drawings.

6. Protection of Materials.

(a) Each part in the structure of the aircraft is to be protected against corrosion or deterioration by an approved method. The aircraft is to be able to withstand satisfactorily the sudden changes in temperature and humidity experienced in semi-tropical climates.

(b) It will be decided either at the mock-up or final examination conference whether the whole or any of the engine or fuselage cowling is to be:-

(i)   Protected against corrosion by the anodic or other approved process, or

(ii) Protected as stated in (I) and afterwards painted so as to render it a non-reflector of light, or

(iii) Left in the polished condition.

Notation shall be made on the relevant drawings in accordance with whatever is decided. Parts coming under head (III) are to be coated with a temporary protective, i.e. lanoline or some other approved substance.

7. Mechanical Tests.

(a) The Contractor will be required to supply specimens of such parts of the aircraft as are considered by the D.T.D. to require testing in order to ensure that the design and construction of the aircraft will be satisfactory.

(b) The tender to this specification is to include a schedule of the specimens and tests considered sufficient to meet the requirements of clause 7(a) and is to cover the cost of supplying and testing the specimens.

(c) The specimens and tests that will probably be essential are indicated hereunder:-

Complete ribs. The specimens are to be tested under the conditions of normal flight and of down load due to gusts.

Metal ribs will be required to undergo, in addition, a vibration test.

Metal spars. The specimens will be submitted to the standard test, if applicable, and otherwise to such test as the D.T.D. may require.

(d) Except as provided for hereafter, the testing shall be done by the Contractor, or he shall arrange for it to be done at some approved Testing Establishment; in either case due notice of the time and place of the tests shall be given to the D.T.D. so that he may arrange for a representative to witness them; the conditions governing the tests are to be in accordance with the requirements of the D.T.D. and the tests are to be performed to his satisfaction; reports on the tests are to be supplied to the D.T.D. in duplicate. If neither of the aforementioned arrangements is possible, the tests will be done at the Royal Aircraft Establishment at the Contractor's expense.

(e) The D.T.D. reserves the right to call for specimens and tests additional to those referred to in the Contractor's schedule, should he at any time after the placing of the contract consider them to be necessary.

(f) No specimen of any part of the aircraft shall be submitted for testing without it having been previously certified by the Inspector-in-Charge at the Contractor's works that the specimen is in accordance with an approved drawing of the part and that the workmanship is satisfactory. Similarly in the case of any specimen that is re-submitted for testing after having been modified.

(g) A thin coat of oil, lanoline or vaseline may be applied to metal specimens to prevent corrosion. Varnish, enamel or similar substances may not be used for this purpose.

8. Power Unit, Etc.

(a) The aircraft shall be fitted with a British engine of a suitable rating. The type of engine may be any which, in the opinion of the D.T.D., is likely to pass the 100 hours Service type test within one year of the submission of tenders to the specification, and for which fuel to specification No. D.T.D. 230 would be suitable. If the selected type is still undergoing development when the tenders are prepared, the design of the aircraft is to allow for possible increases in engine weight. Application should be made to the D.T.D. (R.D.E.) for particulars of the weight, power rating, fuel consumption, etc., of the type of engine selected.

(b) The engine installation arrangements are to be such as will permit of the engine being replaced with ease and rapidity when the aircraft is operating "in the field". It shall be possible for two men to remove and replace the engine in 4 hours. A suitable form of hoist is to be supplied for these purposes, provided that standard tackle cannot be used (see clause 18 (a)). Should an air-cooled radial engine be fitted, it shall be removable complete with bearer plate.

(c) The Contractor should apply to the D.T.D. (R.D.A.4) for an approved engine installation drawing immediately after the contract has been placed.

(d) Supports and footholds are to be provided to facilitate minor repairs and adjustments to the engine and to the installation and accessories.

(e) The engine cowling and any other cowling which will have to be frequently taken off is to be designed so as to facilitate its rapid and easy removal and replacement and is to be sufficiently robust to withstand constant handling (see also clause 6(b)). Wire skewers are not to be used for fastening the cowling.

(f) Before drawings relating to the engine installation can be accepted, the engine, the fuel, oil and engine-cooling systems, and the accessories and piping therefor must be fitted in the aircraft and put in proper running order so that the installation as a whole may be examined and (if satisfactory) approved by the D.T.D. or his authorized representative.

(g) The airscrew shall be satisfactory as regards its strength under the conditions of the diving tests referred to in Aircraft Design Memorandum No. 292 and shall be designed so that it will not permit the engine to exceed:-

- (I) the maximum permissible r.p.m. when the aircraft is flying horizontally, under "full throttle" conditions, at the rated boost pressure at any height, or
- (II) the normal r.p.m. when the aircraft is climbing at the maximum rate, under "full throttle" conditions, at any height above the rated altitude.

(h) Should a wooden 4-blade airscrew be supplied, it shall be of two-part construction.

(i) The tender to this specification is to cover the cost of supplying one spare airscrew.

(j) A standard engine instruction plate is to be fitted in a position where it will be clearly visible to the pilot.

9. Fuel System.

(a) The fuel system shall be designed, constructed, installed and tested in accordance with Specification No. D.T.D.1004. A non-gravity type of system may be provided.

(b) The aggregate capacity of the tanks shall be sufficient for an endurance of 1.25 hours at a height of 20,000 feet (assuming the engine to run continuously at the normal r.p.m.), after allowing for ½ hour with the engine developing the maximum power permissible for continuous running at ground level.

(c) The design of the aircraft shall be such as to facilitate the rapid and easy filling of the tanks, and is to provide for this being done by pumping with a hand pump from bulk containers and directly from tins by hand. Hand and/or footholds are to be provided for the use of a mechanic whilst attending to this operation. In no circumstances shall it be necessary for the purpose of fuelling to employ ladders and/or other gear not forming part of the aircraft's equipment.

(d) Fuel contents gauges are to be installed in positions where they will be clearly visible to the pilot.

10. Oil System.

(a) Pending the issue of Specification No. D.T.D. 1008, which will govern the design, construction, installation and testing of oil systems, the requirements (other than any that are obviously inapplicable) included in Specification No. D.T.D. 1004 under the following headings shall be deemed to apply also to the oil system fitted in the aircraft:-

Materials.

Treatment of materials.

Construction of tanks.

Installation of tanks.

Pipes.

Cocks.

Pressure tests.

(b) The system shall be designed to maintain a satisfactory circulation of the oil at a safe maximum temperature under atmospheric conditions corresponding to those governing the design of the engine-cooling system, and so that there will be no stoppage of the oil supply to the engine when the aircraft is flying in any attitude within limits corresponding to (i) the greatest angle it can reach when taking-off or in climbing flight, and (ii) its angle when diving at the limiting speed.

(c) Provision shall be made for rapidly warming the oil so as to expedite the starting of the engine in cold weather. It is requisite that the aircraft shall be ready to take-off 2½ minutes after starting the engine, assuming both engine and oil to be cold at the start and the air temperature to be 0°c; Corresponding rapidity of starting at air temperatures below 0°c will be advantageous.

(d) The aggregate net capacity of the tanks shall be sufficient for an endurance 2 hours greater than that called for in clause 9(b), plus the "½ hour allowance".

(e) The total capacity of each tank shall include an air-space not less than is indicated hereunder:

Type of Engine.		Airspace (gallons).
Air-cooled	– under 400 H.P.	1
Air-cooled	– between 400 H.P. and 600 H.P.	1 ½
Air-cooled	– over 600 H.P.	2
Water-cooled		
Steam-cooled		2

Note: The horsepowers stated in the case of air-cooled engines are the powers at normal r.p.m.

(f) The system shall include two oil thermometers; one to indicate the temperature of the oil supplied to the engine, the other the temperature of the oil as it leaves the engine (see Aircraft Design Memorandum No. 248). The thermometer scales are to be clearly visible to the pilot and the bulbs are to be completely immersed in the stream of oil.

(g) A gauge to indicate the pressure of the oil in the engine is to be provided in the pilot's cockpit. If an oil cooler is fitted, provision shall be made so that a pressure gauge may be connected to it on the inlet side. (Note: The gauge will be fitted only during the type trials of the aircraft.)

(h) The system shall incorporate a filter, fitted either in the tank sump (as is preferable) or in the pipe from the tank to the engine.

(i) A relief valve or other means of preventing the generation of excessive pressure due to the high viscosity of the oil when cold is to be incorporated in oil coolers.

(j) The risk of fire due to the generation of electricity by friction during re-oiling operations is to be guarded against as prescribed in Aircraft Design Memorandum No. 262.

11. Engine-Starting.

The aircraft is to be equipped with an approved type of starter, which is to be installed in an easily accessible position and is to be operable by the pilot alone without excessive physical exertion.

12. Engine-Cooling.

For air-cooled engines.

(a) Provision is to be made for satisfactory cooling of the engine under temperate conditions.

For water or steam-cooled engines.

(b) An efficient cooling system is to be designed and installed in accordance with the requirements of the D.T.D. The system is to be subjected to a vapour separation test (which shall be performed to the satisfaction of the D.T.D.) and shall provide sufficient cooling to fulfil standard "English Summer" requirements.

(c) A means (preferably automatically-controlled) of regulating the cooling effect is to be provided.

(d) The quantity of reserve water shall not be less than Q gallons, where:

$$Q = 1 + PE/1600$$

P = horsepower of engine at normal r.p.m.

E = required endurance, plus the "½ hour allowance".

The gross capacity of the reserve water tank shall include an air or expansion space of adequate volume.

(e) Except in the case of a tractor aircraft with water-cooled engine, a device designed to give warning when the quantity of reserve water has fallen to the minimum permissible is to be connected to the reserve water tank. The device shall be clearly visible to the pilot.

13. Undercarriage.

(a) The undercarriage is to be retractable and of a type that obviates the use of rubber in tension.

(b) The wheel track is to be of such a width that no risk of overturning will be incurred when the aircraft is manoeuvring on the ground. The aircraft shall be capable of taxying satisfactorily in any direction in a wind of 20 m.p.h.

(c) The dimensions of the wheels and tyres (if of the "high-pressure" type) shall be such that, when the aircraft is standing fully-loaded, the following ratio will not have a value greater than 10:-

$$\frac{\text{Weight supported by each wheel (1b.)}}{\text{Wheel diameter X tyre diameter (ins.)}}$$

(d) A wheel-brake system and a retractable tail wheel are to be fitted. It is desirable that application of the brakes should be effected by means of a hand control on the control columns, and differential action by movement of the rudder bar must be provided for. The wheel is to be limited by movable stops to turning through an angle of 90° to either side of its central position, and shall be designed to permit of a tail steering arm being used.

14. Control Systems, Etc.

(a) The design of the lateral control system is to be such that operation of the ailerons will produce the minimum of adverse yawing effect on the aircraft. Means of ensuring adequate lateral control and stability at and below stalling speed are to be embodied.

(b) A fixed tailplane with adjustable elevator flaps is to be provided. The range of flap adjustment shall be sufficient for coping with normal variations in the load carried, and the control shall be easy to operate throughout this range under all conditions of flight. The change of setting necessary on moving the engine throttle controls from the "fully open" to the "closed" position shall be a minimum.

(c) The range of movement of each control organ is to be limited by stops so that in no circumstances will it jam or foul parts of the aircraft. The stretch of the aileron control circuit shall not exceed that which corresponds to a 18% displacement of the pilot's control lever.

(d) If necessary, provision is to be made for carrying standard ballast to maintain the centre of gravity in its correct position whenever the aircraft is flown not fully loaded. Instructions as to ballasting are to be given on a plate fitted in the aircraft.

(e) A means whereby the pilot may trim the rudder in flight shall be provided.

15. Maintenance.

(a) The construction of component parts of the aircraft is to permit of them being rapidly dismantled, and the aircraft as a whole is to be designed so that the maintenance operations scheduled in Aircraft Design Memorandum No. 242 can be performed quickly and easily and such repair work as R.A.F. Units will be required to undertake can be done with the minimum of difficulty.

(b) Ladders and/or other miscellaneous items which may be necessary in connection with routine maintenance operations are to be supplied with the aircraft as part of its equipment (see paragraph 18).

(c) The design of the aircraft is to provide for it being jacked-up otherwise supported in a secure manner so that the undercarriage or other parts may be removed. The arrangements made for this purpose are not to entail elaborate forms of support or to require that the aircraft be slung. The strong points for jacks and/or trestles are to be easily accessible and clearly marked.

(d) The examination, adjustment and lubrication of all parts of the controls in the planes and elsewhere are to be provided for. So far as may be possible, provision is to be made for the lubrication of moving parts by grease gun from a central nipple, and for the exclusion of dust and water from these parts.

(e) Parts that require frequent inspection or to be frequently replaced are to be easily accessible and fully visible to a mechanic working on them. Provided the type of construction permits, it is desirable that direct access to all such parts in the fuselage should be assured by incorporating a quickly detachable panel or panels (properly sealed at the edges) in the fuselage covering, and that the fuselage and bay should be quickly detachable.

(f) To prevent any need arising for the frequent replacement of pin-jointed parts or for the use of oversize pins or bolts in such parts, the bearing areas for pins or bolts are to be sufficient to prevent the holes elongating under the bearing loads. In addition, in the case of moving parts, wear due to the rotation of pins or bolts is to be provided for by bushing the holes; the bushes are to be easily replaceable.

16. Miscellaneous.

(a) Holding-down rings or the equivalent are to be provided at suitable positions on the aircraft, e.g. the underside of each bottom wing and at the aft end of the fuselage.

(b) Handholes or other aids to the safe and easy handling of the aircraft are to be provided at the tip of each bottom wing and/or at suitable positions on the fuselage. The ingress of water at handholes or other apertures in any covered component is to be guarded against.

(c) The cockpit padding and all other upholstery is to be rendered fireproof to the satisfaction of the D.T.D.

(d) No unapproved kind of safety glass may be used in windscreens or windows.

17. Operational Equipment.

(a) Provisional details of the equipment and parts which are referred to in clause 17(b) and which, under the terms of that clause, it will be necessary for the Contractor to supply and/or fit are given in the Appendix "A" [not included here] which is issued with and forms part of this specification. These details may be amended from time to time during the currency of the contract, in which case notice of such amendments will be given by the Director of Contracts. The aircraft in its completed state is to be equipped in accordance with the Appendix as finally amended.

(b) The aircraft is to be fitted with:-

> (i) the items of equipment forming the typical Military load referred to in clause 19(a);
>
> (ii) the parts necessary in order that any alternative equipment detailed in the Appendix "A" may be carried;
>
> (iii) any parts which may not be included under heads (i) and (ii) but which will be essential in connection with the operation of the aircraft or the use of any of its equipment.

(c) The electrical equipment (if any) is to be installed in accordance with Specification No. G.E. 164.

(d) The aircraft is to be bonded and screened in accordance with Specification No. D.T.D. G.E. 125.

(e) Such parts of the equipment of the aircraft as might (if not specially protected) be accidentally damaged, shall be provided with detachable guards.

(f) The stowage for the signal pistol is to accommodate both the old and the new (light) pattern.

(g) Waterproof covers are to be provided for the engine and airscrew. The design and material of the covers are to be such as will ensure the complete exclusion of water during heavy rainstorms.

(h) Such instruments, plugs and leads as do not form part of the permanent equipment of the aircraft are to have labels affixed to indicate (in the case of instruments) the positions occupied when fitted in the aircraft, or (in the case of plugs and leads) their identities.

(i) On completion of the aircraft the Contractor shall forward to the D.T.D. (R.D.A.4) a copy of the Appendix "A", drafted in accordance with the current master schedule, giving details (weights, lengths and quantities) of the equipment with which the aircraft is fitted.

18. Ancillary Equipment.

(a) The aircraft is to be designed with a view to the fullest possible use being made of standard R.A.F. equipment in connection with the following work:-

    1. Moving the aircraft on the ground.

    2. Filling the tanks.

    3. Routine overhauls of the engine and airframe.

    4. Removing an unserviceable engine.

    5. Jacking-up the aircraft.

Particulars of the standard equipment are obtainable from the D.T.D. (R.D.A.5) on written application being made. Special equipment, including tools, shall be provided with the aircraft if an essential supply, but the introduction of non-standard articles is to be avoided where possible.

(b) Typical items of ancillary equipment which the Contractor may have to supply are as follow:-

    1. Hoist for engine-changing.

    2. Ladders for reaching the engine and tanks and controls in the top plane.

    3. Undercarriage jacks.

    4. Wing and tail trestles.

    5. Tail steering arm.

(c) The tender to this specification is to include a schedule of the non-standard equipment which is considered essential and is to cover the cost of such equipment. A decision as to the equipment to be provided will be given at the mock-up conference.

19. Typical Load.

(a) The total load to be carried by the aircraft for the purpose of the type trials referred to in paragraph 24 shall comprise:-

    (i) the military load specified hereunder, together with such removable non-standard parts as it will be necessary for the Contractor to supply and fit in that this military load may be carried;

    (ii) fuel for the endurance specified in clause 9(b), plus the "½ hour allowance";

    (iii) oil and cooling water for an endurance 2 hours greater than that called for in clause 9(b), plus the "½ hour allowance";

    (iv) the "tare weight" items shown in column 10 of the Appendix "A".

<u>Military Load.</u>
(weight of crew and removable standard items only)

Item No.	Item.	Weight (1b.).
1	Pilot.	180
2	Parachute.	20
3	<u>Armament</u>:	
	(a) Browning guns (8).	164
	(b) S.A.A. (2,400 rounds).	174
4	<u>Instruments.</u>	
	(a) Navigational.	0.5
	(b) Oxygen apparatus.	12
5	R/T. apparatus (T.R.9).	50
6	Signal pistol and 8 cartridges.	6.5
	TOTAL:	607 1bs.

(b) The weight of the aircraft, fully-loaded, is defined as its weight when carrying the total load referred to in clause 19(a) or any alternative load weighing the same as the said load, and references elsewhere in the specification to the aircraft in its "fully loaded" condition shall be construed accordingly.

20. Structural Strength, Etc.

(a) The strength of the aircraft when flying in the fully loaded condition shall not be less than is defined by the factors stated hereunder:-

1. Load factor throughout the structure with the centre of pressure in its most forward position in normal flight 10.0

2. Load factor for the wing structure with the centre of pressure in its most backward position in horizontal (normal) flight 7.5

3. Factor of safety throughout the structure in a dive to the terminal speed with the tail plane at any setting down to the most negative at which it is estimated that the aircraft could be held in the dive 2.2

4. Load factor for the wing structure under a gust (either up or down) of 25 feet/second when the aircraft is flying at its normal top speed 2.0

5. Load factor for the wing structure at the angle of incidence corresponding to an inverted stall with the centre of pressure at 0.33 of the chord 5.0

6. Load factor for the wing structure at the angle of incidence corresponding to an inverted glide at a speed equal to the normal top speed in horizontal (normal) flight 5.0

7. Factor of safety for the wing structure in a dive to the terminal speed, assuming any one wire to be cut 1.1

(b) The aircraft, fully-loaded, shall be able to withstand an impact with the ground at a vertical velocity of 10 feet per second, and at this velocity the impact load on the under carriage is not to exceed three times the weight of the aircraft, fully-loaded. The load factor for the undercarriage when subject to this impact load shall not be less than 1.5 and for the remainder of the structure not less than 1.7 (this difference between load factors is always to be maintained whatever modifications may eventually be made in the design of the experimental aircraft). The factors of safety when the aircraft is at rest on the ground shall not be less that the following:-

Factor of safety for the undercarriage 4.4

Factor of safety for the remainder of the aircraft 5.0

The factor of safety throughout the structure under a side load at the axle equal to the weight of the aircraft, fully-loaded, shall not be less than 1.1.

(c) The factors referred to in clauses 20(a) and 20(b) can be taken as ultimate factors and are to be determined by methods approved by the D.T.D.

(Note: Application of "strain energy" principles in the strength calculations will not entail an increase in these factors.) Each component is to be designed so that, under a load equal to 75% of the maximum factored load it has to resist, it will suffer no deformation that would render the aircraft unairworthy. Should the actual factors for any part of the aircraft prove to be less than those specified herein, a compensatory addition (equal to the estimated weight, as agreed between the D.T.D. and the Contractor, of the reinforcement necessary to remedy the deficiency) will be made to the load to be carried during the type trials.

(d) The torsional and flexural stiffnesses of the wings, fuselage and tail unit shall be satisfactory under the worst conditions likely to be encountered. In calculating stiffnesses the contribution from fabric covering is to be disregarded. The Contractor shall provide facilities at his works for stiffness measurements to be made; before and after covering if fabric is used for this purpose.

(e) The reserve factor for the fittings by which the safety belt is attached to the aircraft shall not be less than 1, assuming that simultaneous accelerations of 7g. forward and parallel to the thrust line and 5g upward and normal to the thrust line are imposed on the pilot (who shall be assumed to weigh 200 lb. depending on whether or not his parachute is of the "seat" type). Where the belt is anchored to a seat, the reserve factor for the seat and the fittings which attach it to the aircraft shall not be less than 1.5 times the reserve factor for the belt fittings.

(f) The fuselage structure in the vicinity of the cockpit is to be designed to afford the pilot as much protection as possible in the event of a heavy landing or crash. Such structure shall be appreciably stronger than the adjacent parts so that these latter will absorb some of the shock by deformation before the former yields. Suitable structure is to be provided to ensure that the pilot will not be imprisoned or severely injured should the aircraft turn over when landing.

(g) Satisfactory anchorages are to be provided for all such items of equipment as would, in the event of a heavy landing or crash, be liable to break from their positions and injure the pilot. The strength of the anchorages is to be at least as great as that of the structure to which they are attached under forward inertia forces acting parallel to the thrust line.

(h) The factor of safety (based on ultimate strength) for platforms or similar parts included in the aircraft structure or for any item of ancillary equipment supplied by the Contractor for lifting or supporting an engine, freight, personnel, etc., shall not be less than 4. If the item is so constructed that its strength cannot be accurately calculated from existing data, it shall be subjected to a proof load equal to twice the maximum static load it is required to withstand. The inscription "Safe for loads up to (here insert the maximum static load figure)" is to be painted or otherwise marked on each such item at a clearly visible point.

(i) The tail wheel shall be capable of withstanding loads occasioned by sudden application of the brakes and abrupt changes in the aircraft's direction of motion.

(j) The ailerons and the fittings for their attachment shall have a factor of safety not less than 1.5 under the loads produced by sudden movement of the ailerons up or down through the greatest angle possible or 20° (whichever is the lesser) when the aircraft is in horizontal flight at its maximum speed.

(k) The detail requirements (where appropriate) of Air Publication No. 970 are to be satisfied.

21. Final Examination.

(a) The Contractor shall provide facilities at his works for a final examination of the aircraft in its completed or nearly-completed state to be made on behalf of the D.T.D. in order that it may be seen (i) whether the aircraft is suitable as regards its construction and equipment for the stated purpose and satisfies the requirements of the D.T.D. or (ii) whether any alterations will be necessary prior to the commencement of the type trials. This examination shall take place as soon as possible after the aircraft has passed the final inspection required by the Director of Aeronautical Inspection.

(b) The aircraft is to be presented for examination equipped in accordance with the requirements stated in or implied by paragraphs 17 and 19, unless (see clause 21(c)) these requirements are varied after the contract for the aircraft has been placed. If so required, the Contractor shall subsequently take out the removable equipment forming part of the load defined in clause 19(a) and shall install the alternative items of removable equipment that are detailed in the Appendix "A", or he shall demonstrate that these alternative items can be installed in a satisfactory manner.

(c) The requirements referred to in the two preceding clauses shall be deemed to consist of (i) those stated in this specification, and (ii) all supplementary and/ or amended requirements (if any) of which the Contractor is given separate notice by the Director of Contracts prior to the final examination.

(d) Items of non-standard ancillary equipment supplied by the Contractor in accordance with paragraph 18 are to be available at the final examination of the aircraft, and if so required the Contractor shall demonstrate their use.

(e) The Contractor will be notified by the Director of Contracts of all alterations required to be made to the aircraft and ancillary equipment consequent upon the final examination, and shall complete these alterations to the satisfaction of the D.T.D.

22. Weight and Centre of Gravity.

(a) The Contractor shall furnish to the D.T.D. or his authorised representative (at least one week before the aircraft will be delivered to the official test station for type trials) written particulars of:-

  (i)   the tare weight of the aircraft and

  (ii) its weight and the position of its centre of gravity when fully-loaded (unless it is likely that the aircraft will be delivered for the trials in an incompletely equipped state, when the parts of which it is expected to be deficient shall be clearly designated, but their weights left out of account).

(b) The tare weight of the aircraft is its weight when fitted with the fixed equipment detailed in column 10 of the Appendix "A" but not with any removable equipment, and with the fuel and oil tanks empty. In the case of aircraft with water or evaporatively-cooled engines, the weight of the cooling water is to be included in the tare weight.

(c) The Contractor will be required to certify that the methods whereby the weight and centre of gravity have been determined are such that:-

  (i)   the stated weight is accurate to within 0.2 per cent;

  (ii) the stated C.G. co-ordinate parallel to the datum line (see Aircraft Design Memorandum No. 205), is accurate to within 1 per cent of the mean chord dimension;

  (iii) the stated C.G., co-ordinate normal to the datum line is accurate to within 5 per cent of the mean chord dimension.

No methods that entail weighing in the open will be allowed.

(d) On or before completion of the aircraft the Contractor shall forward to the D.T.D. (R.D.A.S.) an analysis of the weights of its constituent parts, etc. A form suitable for the analysis will be issued to the Contractor at or about the time when the contract is placed.

23. Pre-Acceptance Test Flights.

Prior to the delivery of the aircraft it shall have been certified to the D.T.D. by the Contractor:-

(i) that the aircraft has been subjected by the Contractor's pilot to the following tests:-

1. Full acrobatic flying tests in accordance with Aircraft Design Memorandum No. 291.

2. Diving tests in accordance with Aircraft Design Memorandum No. 292.

3. Full spinning tests in accordance with Aircraft Design Memorandum No. 293.

4. General flight trials in accordance with Aircraft Design Memorandum No. 294.

5. Lateral stability tests in accordance with Aircraft Design Memorandum No. 295.

(ii) that the abovementioned tests have shown that the aircraft is safe to be flown by Royal Air Force pilots.

24. Performance, Stability and Control.

(a) The performance of the aircraft (as ascertained by official type trials), when fitted with an airscrew satisfying the requirements of clause 8(g) and loaded in accordance with clause 19(a) (subject to such adjustments as may be required in accordance with clause 20(c)), shall reach the standards indicated hereunder:-

1. The maximum speed at an altitude of 15,000 feet shall not be less than 275 m.p.h. and at 5,000 feet not less than 250 m.p.h.

2. Endurance – as stated in clause 9(b).

3. The time taken to reach 20,000 feet is not to exceed 7¼ minutes.

4. The service ceiling is to be not less than 33,000 feet.

5. The distance from (a) the point at which the aircraft during its approach in a straight glide to land (in still air) would just clear a 50-foot screen, to (b) the point at which it comes to root, shall not exceed 600 yards, and the length of the landing run shall not exceed 250 yards.

(b) The aircraft, when flying fully-loaded, shall:-

(i) have positive stability about all axes;

(ii) be fully controllable at any speed, especially near the stall and during a steep dive, when it shall have no tendency to hunt;

(iii) respond quickly to the controls and be easy to manoeuvre, whatever its speed may be, provided that this shall not be realized at the expense of performance;

(iv) not be tiring to fly;

(v) form a steady platform for firing at any speed up to its terminal speed;

(vi) not experience excessive fluctuations in the speed for which it is trimmed if the throttle is moved from the correct position for that speed to any other position.

It is also to satisfy the foregoing requirements as completely as possible when carrying any permissible load.

(c) Effective longitudinal control is to be available at all speeds from the limiting speed to below the stalling speed.

(d) The aircraft shall be such that it can be readily put into a spin and that in recovering from spins it satisfies the requirements of Aircraft Design Memorandum No. 293.

25. Drawing, Etc. To Be Supplied.

(a) Drawings of the lay-out as provisionally arranged at the mock-up conference are to be submitted by the Contractor in duplicate to the D.T.D. (R.D.A.4) not later than 10 days after the conference. Drawings of the lay-out as arranged for final approval are to be supplied in quadruplicate. These drawings are to be a 1/8th scale and are to comprise (i) skeleton views of the fuselage and other pertinent structure showing:-

1. the equipment positioned on the starboard side, viewed from inside;
2. the equipment positioned on the port side, viewed from inside;
3. the equipment viewed in plan;

and (ii) full views of instrument boards, R/T panels, etc., and (iii) a schedule of equipment indexed to correspond to "balloon" pointers on the drawings; the schedule is to include a spare column for notes and alternations. Each drawing is also to show the seats, tanks, controls and/or other parts appropriate to the view.

(b) As soon as possible after the mock-up conference the Contractor shall supply to the Resident Technical Officer for transmission to the D.T.D. (R.D.A.4 and Airworthiness Dept.) full particulars (in duplicate, including duplicate copies of the drawings and/or diagram necessary) of the fuel, oil and engine-cooling systems.

(c) As soon as possible after the aircraft has been built the Contractor is to submit the "Type Record", i.e. a detailed description of the aircraft, such drawings as may be required, a summary of the strength calculations and detailed weight data, to the D.T.D. or his representative for acceptance.

(d) When the aircraft is handed over for type trials, copies of the General Arrangement drawings of the completed aircraft shall be forwarded, with General Arrangement drawings showing the lay-out of the whole of the equipment, to the D.T.D. (R.D.A.4) in duplicate, and similarly for any subsequent aircraft, if different from the first.

(e) The following are to be supplied in accordance with the Director of Contracts' circular letter, reference 163625/32/C.4(a).

1. Descriptive Notes and Rigging Instructions.
2. Maintenance Schedule.
3. Repair Notes.

26. Models.

(a) In order that a model of the aircraft may be constructed for test of its spinning characteristics, the Contractor shall supply to the D.T.D. (Airworthiness Dept.), as soon as possible after the contract has been placed, drawings (in duplicate) showing:-

(i)   its general arrangement in front elevation, side elevation and plan;
(ii) its wing section(s);
(iii) the distribution of its mass relative to each of the three principal axes;
(iv) the position of its centre of gravity.

The Contractor shall forward with the abovementioned drawings a completed Aerodynamic Data Sheet, a proforma of which will be supplied to him at or about the time the contract is placed by the D.T.D. (R.D.A.3).

(b) If so required at any time by the D.T.D. the Contractor shall furnish the drawings and data necessary in connection with the construction of a true-to-scale model of the complete aircraft for test in a wind tunnel.

27. Publication of Test Results.

The D.T.D. reserves the right to publish data contained in reports of any wind tunnel or other tests relating to the design of the aircraft that may be undertaken on his behalf.

D.T.D.,
AIR MINISTRY.

AEROPLANE AND ARMAMENT EXPERIMENTAL ESTABLISHMENT.
MARTLESHAM HEATH.
HAWKER MONOPLANE, F.36/34 K-5083.
MERLIN C.
A. & A.E.E. Ref:- N/4482/30 A.S.55

A. N. Ref:- 385627/35/R.D.A.1/F.E.C.

In accordance with the instructions received in Air Ministry letter, reference 385627/35/R.D.A., dated 16.12.35 short performance and handling trials have been made, the results of which are given in the accompanying pages.

FORM 897.

TEST REPORT No. M/689

Date. April 1936.

AEROPLANE. Hawker Monoplane   No. K-5083.

ENGINE TYPE. Merlin C.

SPECIFICATION. No. F.36/34   DUTY. High speed single seater fighter.

CONTRACTOR. Hawker Aircraft Ltd.

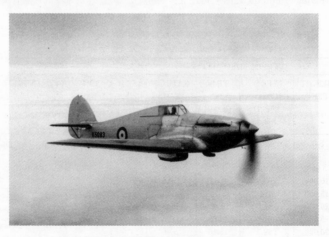

The prototype K5083 in flight, c.1937.

SUMMARY OF TRIALS.

Tests reduced on the basis $\rho \frac{1}{2} \sigma \frac{1}{2}$

AEROPLANE   Hawker Monoplane   No. K-5083

SPEC. No. F. 36/34.

CONTRACT. 357483/34.

CONTRACTOR. Hawker Aircraft Ltd.

TYPE   Landplane   DUTY   High Speed Single Seater Fighter.

ENGINE. Merlin C   Normal B. H. P. 1029 at Rated Altitude / 11, 000 ft.

        No. 111144   "   "   "   "   "

At   2600   R. P. M.   at rated boost pressure 46 lb/sq.in.

"   "

                                              lb.

Tare weight

Weight light

Fixed military load

Service load

Fuel (firm's figure) 107.5 gallons*

Oil ("   ")   7

Flying weight on trials – 5672 lb.

*Based on 7.7. lb. per gallon.

AT FULL THROTTLE				ECONOMICAL SPEED			
HEIGHT FEET	TRUE AIR TOP SPEED M.P.H. Kts.	TIME TO CLIMB Mins.	RATE OF CLIMB Ft./Min.	M.P.H. Kts.	R.P.M. (Mean)	RANGE	
						MILES LAND SEA	HOURS
S.L.	253	0	2550				
2,000	261.5	0.76	2650				
5,000	274	1.89	2810				
10,000	295.5	3.63	2680				
15,000	314	5.70	2150				
20,000	311	8.40	1620				
25,000	301.5	12.08	1100				
30,000	282.5	18.10	570				

Service ceiling (estimated) 34,500 ft.   Landing speed (from camera) 50 M.P.H. KTS.

Take off run 265 yds. Time. 11 ½ secs. (flaps shut) (flaps open)

Distance from rest to clear 50 ft. Screen 430 yds.

Stalling speed (A.S.I.) 57 M.P.H. KTS.

Gliding in A.S.I. 78 M.P.H. KTS.

BEST Landing A.S.I. 70 M.P.H. KTS.

Distance to rest (with brakes) (flaps open) 475 yds.

after clearing 50 ft. screen yds.

Landing and take off tests corrected to wind of 5 m.p.h.

In view of the urgency of the trials and as the aircraft was received ballasted by the firm to represent from the weight and C.G. point of view the aircraft with 8 gun wings and other service equipment, no attempt was made to weight the aircraft light or determine the tank capacities. It should be noted that the ballast to represent the guns was carried in the fuselage.

WEIGHTS AND LOADING DATA.

(in accordance with Weight Sheet Summary Serial No. A. P. Vol. III., Part 3.

As loaded by makers:-

	lb.
Tare weight	-
Weight light	-
Fixed military load	-
Service load	-
Fuel (full)	-
Oil (full)	-
Flying weight on trials	-
Maximum capacity of tanks:-	5672
Fuel 107.5	gallons.

Firm's figures.

Oil 8   gallons.

ITEMS.	FIXED MILITARY LOAD.	SERVICE LOAD.
1. Crew		
2. Gun load		200
3. Bomb load		
4. Torpedo load		
5. Pyrotechnic load		
6. Electrical load		
7. Instrument load		
8. Miscellaneous load		
9. Wireless		
TOTALS	(A).........lb.	(B).........lb.

TOTAL MILITARY LOAD (A) + (B)   lb.

CENTRE OF GRAVITY with above load, including C. G. limits.

The centre of gravity with the above load is at 51.2" aft of the datum point.

The provisional centre of gravity limits to cover expenditure of fuel and oil are 50.0" and 51.7" aft of the datum point.

The datum point is the centre of the engine starting handle shaft. The datum line is the rigging datum line.

DIRECTION OF ROTATION

Direction of rotation
R.H. Tractor.
POSITION Centre.
TYPE Blade Wood.
MARKINGS C.3612
Drg.No.Watts Z.3300/1.
WEIGHT 96½ lb.

	MARKED	MEASURED
PITCH	20.5 ft	20.57ft
DIA.	11.5ft	11.52ft

RADIUS INS.	CHORD INS.	ANGLE	THICKNESS INS.
	14.44	42°10'	2.0
41.35	14.39	42°4'	2.0
(0.7 RAD)	13.28	39°14'	1.62
	13.24	39°2'	1.65
48.4			
	12.35	37°56'	1.40
51.73	12.34	37°54'	1.40
62.1	7.82	33°34'	0.77
	7.77	33°20'	0.78

Note: a drawing of the airscrew was not supplied.

CLIMBING TRIALS.

HEIGHT IN STANDARD ATMOS-PHERE. Feet	TIME FROM START. Min.	RATE OF CLIMB. Ft./Min.	TRUE AIR SPEED. M.P.H.	A.S.I. M.P.H.	POSITION ERROR CORREC-TION. and # Compress-ibility Correction	R.P.M.	BOOST. lb/sq.in.	RADIATOR.
Sea Level	0	2550	151.5	150	+1.5 0	2100	+6	
1,000	0.38	2600	154	150	+1.5 0	2125	+6	
2,000	0.76	2650	156	150	+1.5 0	2155	+6	
3,000	1.15	2710	158.5	150	+1.5 0	2180	+6	
5,000	1.89	2810	163.5	150	+1.5 0	2235	+6	
6,500	2.43	2880	167	150	+1.5 0	2275	+6	
10,000	3.63	2680	173.5	148	+1.6 – 0.5	2305	+4.15	
13,000	4.8	2370	177.5	144	+1.9 – 0.5	2305	+2.25	
15,000	5.7	2150	181	142	+2.0 – 0.5	2305	+1.1	
16,500	6.4	2000	183	140	+2.1 – 0.5	2300	+0.3	
18,000	7.25	1840	186.5	139	+2.2 – 0.5	2300	–0.5	
20,000	8.4	1620	189.5	136.5	+2.3 – 0.5	2295	–1.5	
23,000	10.4	1310	195	133	+2.5 – 0.5	2285	–2.9	
26,000	13.0	990	199.5	129.5	+2.7 – 1.0	2265	–4.3	
28,000	15.2	790	204	127.5	+2.9 – 1.0	2245	-	
30,000	18.1	570	208	125	+3.0 – 1.0	2210	-	
7,600	2.76	2950	170	150	+1.5 0	2300	+6	

Estimated absolute ceiling. 35,400 ft.   Greatest height reached 30,000 ft.
R. P. M. stationary on ground. 1990   Boost pressure lb./sq.in. +6
#Additional correction to allow for air compressibility effect on A.S.I. reading.
*Full throttle height.

SPEED TRIALS.

HEIGHT IN STANDARD ATMOSPHERE. Feet	TRUE AIR SPEED. M.P.H.	A.S.I. M.P.H.	POSITION ERROR COR- RECTION. and Compressibility (See note 1) Correction.	R.P.M.	BOOST. lb./sq.in.	Approx. True Air SPEED AT 2570 R.P.M.
Sea	253	258	−4.9 0	2505	+6	
Level	257.5	259	−5.0 0	2535	+6	
1,000	251.5	259.5	−5.0 −0.3	2560	+6	
2,000	265.5	259.5	−5.0 −0.4	2590	+6	
3,000	274	260	−5.0 −0.7	2645	+6	
5,000	280.5	260.5	−5.0 −1.0	2685	+6	
6,500	295.5	260.5	−5.0 −1.7	2785	+6	
10,000	308	259.5	−5.0 −2.3	2870	+6	
13,000	314	256.5	−4.8 −2.7	2930	+6	
15,000	315	251	−4.5 −2.8	2960	+5.7	273
16,500	313.5	243.5	−4.1 −2.9	2940	+4.3	
18,000	311	233.4	−3.4 −3.1	2910	+2.7	
20,000	306	217.5	−2.4 −3.1	2860	+0.55	
23,000	298.5	201	−1.5 −2.9	2795	−1.4	
26,000	291.5	188.5	−0.8 −2.7	2745	−2.65	
30,000	282.5	175	0 −2.5	2680	−3.90	
15,200	315	252	−4.5 −2.9	2960	+6.0	

Landing and take off tests corrected to wind of 5 m.p.h.

Take off run (flaps shut) 255 yds. Time 1 ½ secs.

Distance from rest to clear 50 foot screen 430 yds.

Gliding in A.S.I. 78 M.P.H. Stalling speed flaps shut 77 M.P.H.

Best landing A.S.I. 70 M.P.H. open 57 M.P.H./A.S.I

Distance to rest (with brakes) after passing over 50 ft. screen 475 yds.

Landing run with brakes 205 yds. Landing run without brakes 525 yds.

Note: The landing runs quoted are with flaps open.

Take-off airspeed from camera measurements 81 m.p.h.

Landing   ”   ”   ”   ” 59 m.p.h.

#Additional correction to allow for air compressibility effect on A.S.I. reading.

*Full throttle height.

HANDLING TRIALS.

The handling trials were made with the aircraft loaded to a total weight of 5572 lb., the position of the Centre of Gravity at the start of flight being 51.2 inches art of the datum point.

As the present Centre of Gravity range of movement is very small, and is only representative of the change as fuel and oil are consumed, no attempt was made to test the aircraft loaded for the start of its flight at any other centre of Gravity position than that quoted above.

Controls.

Ailerons.

The aileron controls operate freely and without play when the aircraft is on the ground; and full sideways movement of the control column can be obtained when the pilot is in the cockpit.

In the air the ailerons are light to handle at low speed when climbing and on the glide, but increase in speed results in a steady increase in heaviness; and at maximum level speed and in the dive the aileron control is heavy for a fighting aircraft. A small peculiarity in the control is that, at moderate speeds only, when the starboard aileron is raised the feel suddenly becomes slightly lighter and the control more effective.

The response to the ailerons is rapid and they are effective under all normal manoeuvres in flight. During landing, take-off and at the stall the response is less rapid and the ailerons less effective and both remain satisfactory.

In general it is considered that the aileron control is satisfactory for a fighting aircraft. If it could be made lighter at high speeds without over-balancing it would be improved.

Rudder.

On the ground the rudder control operates freely and without undue play. In the air it is light at low speeds with engine on and on the glide. With engine on heaviness increases considerably with increase of speed and in the dive it is extremely heavy.

Response is quick and the control is effective at all speeds and under all conditions of flight.

In general it is considered that the rudder control is adequate but would be considerably improved if it could be made lighter at speeds over 150 m.p.h.

Rudder Bias Gear.

The rudder bias control is quick and easy to operate and effective. The range of control is just adequate when the trimming strip on the rudder has been correctly adjusted.

Elevators.

On the ground full movement of the elevators can be obtained without undue friction or play.

In the air the elevator controls are light and effective. They give a quick response under all conditions of flight from the stall to diving speeds. The control is quite satisfactory and suitable.

Tail Trimming Gear.

The tail trimming gear is easy and rapid in operation and has no tendency to slip. Range of control is not quite adequate to trim the aircraft for every condition of flight. A slight increase in the range at both ends of the scale may prove necessary to allow for change in the centre of gravity position. The operating cables are inclined to stretch, allowing some free movement to the trimming tabs and giving an unpleasant effect of fore and aft instability.

Tail Setting.

Loading	Engine on.			Engine off.
	Climbing at beat speed.	Maximum level flight	Specification Cruising Speed	Beat approach speed.
Full load with corresponding C.G.	Full forward.	Not quite full forward.	Not quite full forward.	Fully back.
C.G. Forward		Not Tested.		
C.G. AFT.		Not Tested.		

Engine Controls.

The engine controls are well placed in the cockpit and operate without play or tendency to slip.

Flaps.

The flap control gear is well placed in the cockpit. Is easy to operate and takes 10 to 15 seconds to move ever the full range.

Although there is a noticeable change of trim with flaps down, the tail trimming gear need not be adjusted until the flaps are fully down as the elevator control is powerful enough to counteract the change in trim.

The flaps are very effective and, when down, give improved aileron control. Use of flaps make the approach very simple and reduces flatness of glide. If the throttle is opened when the flaps are lowered the aeroplane will maintain height.

Brakes.

Brakes are smooth, progressive, effective, and easy to operate; but care must be exercised towards the end of the landing run to avoid tipping the aircraft on its nose.

FLYING QUALITIES.

Stability.

Laterally the aircraft is stable. It tends to fly left wing down on the climb and right wing down at top speed.

Directionally the aircraft is stable under all conditions of flight with engines on and off.

Longitudinally the aircraft is neutrally stable with engine on and stable with engine off for the centre of gravity position tested.

Characteristics at the Stall.

The stall is normal with no vice nor any snatching at the controls.

Aerobatics.

Loops, half rolls off loops and stalled turns have been carried out. The aircraft handles well at moderate or slow speeds, but at high speeds, the aerobatic handling would be improved by a lighter rudder and ailerons.

Landing and Take-off.

The aircraft is easy and normal to take-off and to land. There is a tendency to swing to the left when taking off but this can easily be counteracted by the rudder. There is no swing when landing.

If the engine is opened up with the undercarriage down and with tail trimming gear and flaps set for landing the aircraft can still be held by the elevator control.

Sideslipping.

The aircraft is difficult to sideslip and cannot be held in a sustained sideslip beyond about 10°.

Ground handling.

The aircraft is easy to handle on the ground and stable in winds up to 30 m.p.h.

UNDERCARRIAGE.

The undercarriage is very satisfactory having good shock absorbing qualities and good rebound damping. The retracting gear is simple and easy to operate. The undercarriage can be retracted in about 45 seconds without undue exertion by the pilot, and it can be lowered in about 20 seconds. The indicator works satisfactorily and the wheels themselves can be retracted in about 45 seconds without undue exertion by the pilot, and it can be lowered in about 20 seconds. The indicator works satisfactorily and the wheels themselves can be seen, when up or down, through small windows in the floor. This latter is an excellent feature.

FLYING VIEW.

The view forwards and around the upper hemisphere is good except that there is one small blind spot aft which obscures the tail and rudder. In a fighting aircraft view in this direction may be important, though for Home Defence purposes less important, and if this blind spot could be eliminated the fighting view would be much improved. View downwards is largely blanked by the wings, but the view for take-off and landing is good. The covered cockpit enables the pilot to look aft without risk of having his goggles blown off.

COCKPIT COMFORT.

The cockpit is extremely roomy and comfortable and keeps warm even down to -50°C. It is not unduly noisy and the layout of instruments and controls is satisfactory.

The cockpit is easy to enter and leave when the aircraft is on the ground and the roof is fully open.

It was found that at speeds above approximately 150 m.p.h. it was impossible to slide the cockpit roof to the open position and at these speeds the air pressure will slide the cockpit roof from the open to the closed position.

Consequently it is quite impossible for the pilot to make an emergency exit at any speed above 150 m.p.h., and it is submitted that this is a defect unacceptable in a high speed, fighting aircraft. Modification is required to the cockpit roof so that it can be opened at any speed.

DIVING AND STABILITY TESTS.

A diving test was made with the aircraft loaded as described.

The limiting conditions for the dives were 3150 r.p.m. or an indicated airspeed of 300 m.p.h., whichever occurred first.

The observations made during the dives are given in the following table:-

Height in Pt.	Max. A.S.I. m.p.h.	Max. R. P. L.	Height out Pt.	Throttle Setting.
14,000	280	2700	12,500	Fully open
14,000	310	2800	8,000	⅔ open.
14,000	310	2700	8,000	⅓ open.

The aircraft was steady in the dives and small movements of the controls led to the correct response without any signs of control surface instability or vibration.

Recovery was easily effected in all cases.

The heaviness of the aileron and rudder controls under diving conditions is referred to under "Controls".

DESIGN AND CONSTRUCTION.

With the exception of damage sustained by the port undercarriage due to the lack of clearance of the collapsible fairing, no trouble has been experienced with the airframe at this Establishment.

The damage (mentioned above) was caused by the fairing striking a tuft of earth and grass roots on landing. This damage, whilst not affecting the actual structure of the undercarriage, resulted in a fracture of the pipe line to the brakes. It is suggested, therefore, that when the collapsible fairings are modified to give more clearance, the pipe line be fitted to the oleo leg structure and not to the fairing.

POWER UNIT AND INSTALLATION.

Report under the following Heading:- Fuel System.

The aircraft arrived with Merlin 'C' No. 15 installed. During flight tests by the firm's pilot, F/Lt. Bulman, high oil temperatures occurred. It was suspected at the time that the thermostatic by-pass valve in the oil system was at fault, but after removing and coating, it was found to be satisfactory. It was thought, therefore, that the high oil temperature complained about was due to the oil radiator freezing up and the oil by-passing.

Following a further flight test ground running indicated that some major failure had occurred and an inspection of the engine showed that the supercharger tail bearing had failed. The engine was removed and the supercharger extracted and it was found then that both the tail and roller bearings had failed.

A new engine was fitted and a test flight of 1 hour 20 minutes was carried out, but cutting out occurred on 'B' side magneto. This magneto was replaced by a new one, further flight tests showed that the engine running was now fairly satisfactory up to 10,000 ft. During the next flight the firm's test pilot complained of rough running, outing cut, and oily exhaust. General inspection of the engine indicated piston failure. The engine was removed and merlin 'C' No. 19 installed in its place. A test flight was carried out, but the inlet oil temperature rose to 90°. Examination of the aircraft after the flight showed that some grit had entered the thermostatic by-pass valve which accounted for the trouble. Later further rough running developed, also pepping back in the carburettor.

Messrs. Rolls-Royce carried out a number of modifications to the carburation system and a number of types of plugs were tried. At the end of the tests it was apparent that Lodge A. 14D/1 were the only suitable plugs available. Also it was found that it was essential to use magnetos having no safety gap, and unbraided H.T. cables.

At the 20-hour inspection of this engine it was found that three outer and one inner valve springs were broken.

In addition to the above failures two failures occurred to the outcastle boost control, the failures being due to the capsules collapsing. The faulty capsules were made by Messrs Smiths.

During the tests by service pilots, the engine cut out several times and on each occasion it was noted that a complete cut-out occurred after approximately 1 hour 10 minutes flying.

On subsequent examination of the fuel tanks it was found that the port tank was empty, the aircraft having been flown with all tanks "on".

An investigation in the system indicated that the cutting out was due to vapour locks in the petrol system, and special instructions were given to the pilots in order to avoid uncovering the tank outlet. Following the issue of those instructions there was no further cutting out from this cause. As far as can be seen the system as it stands is unsatisfactory. With both wing tanks "on" there is nothing to ensure that they empty simultaneously, and should either empty before the other system is such that the pump is certain to suck in air.

It was doubted at first whether there was sufficient head on the gravity tank to open the non-return valve against the pressure of the engine pumps. A flight test, however, with both wing tanks "off" showed that the gravity tank did actually feed the carburettor as intended.

As however it is understood that this engine is not of the type which will be fitted to the production aircraft, the modifications and adjustments made were only such as to ensure satisfactory running for the purposes of the flight tests.

It is considered that the carburation of the engine at present is unsatisfactory for service use, the running being far too sensitive to slight mixture adjustments.

SUMMARY OF FLYING QUALITIES.

The aircraft is simple and easy to fly and has no apparent vices. All controls operate satisfactorily and are excellent at low speeds. Aileron and rudder control become too heavy at high speeds.

Take off and landing present no difficulty and, in spite of the high top speed, there is no difficulty in making an approach into a normal aerodrome when the undercarriage and flaps are down.

EXTRACTS FROM ENGINE LOG BOOK.
(PROVISIONAL RATING)
ENGINE.

Type. Merlin.   Mk. No. C.

Makers No. 19   A No. 111144

Rating of Engine at   }   Normal R.P.M. 2600 B.H.P. 950

                           }

Rated Altitude 11,000 ft. }   Maximum R.P.M 3000 B.H.P.

Boost pressures. Rated +6 lb/sq. in. Max. Permissible +6 lb/sq. in.

Power curve   R.P.M.: 3000 : 2800 : 2600 : 2400 :   2200   :

----

at 11, 000 ft. B.H.P.: 1189 : 1129 : 1029 : 905 :   780   :

Fuel used during test D.T.D. 230

Acceptance test consumption .606 pts/HP/Hr.

Oil used during test D.T.D.109.

Acceptance test consumption 32 pts/Hr.

Gear ratio   .477   :1.

Total hours run 9 hours 30 minutes when received at this Establishment.

Date power curve taken 22.2.36.

Reference No. 526405/36/R.D.A.3.

AIR MINISTRY.
Directorate of Technical Development.
Confidential.

Specification No. 15/36.
Hawker "Hurricane".
Development – Production.

Specification of <u>Particular Requirements to accompany the Contract Agreement.</u>

This Specification is to be regarded for contract purposes as forming part of the Contract Agreement and being subject to the same conditions.

Approved by:

(Sgd.) R.H. Verney,

Deputy Director, for Director of Technical Development.

Date: 20th July, 1936.

I. General.

(a) The aircraft are to be constructed in strict accordance with the drawings and schedules covering the design, construction, etc., of the experimental aircraft K.5083, in the form in which that aircraft is accepted by the Director of Technical Development as the prototype of the production aircraft, except as modified by other requirements of this specification, or by detail alterations accepted by the D.T.D. to facilitate production.

(b) The Contractor shall furnish descriptive notes and rigging instructions, a maintenance schedule, and instructions for repair, in accordance with the Director of Contracts' letter reference 163625/32/C.4. (a).

(c) Airscrews are only to be supplied if called for in the contract schedule.

2. Interchangeability.

(a) Provision is to be made for the interchangeability of component parts of the aircraft structure in accordance with Specification No. D.T.D.1019. Main components are to be built upon jigs which will ensure their interchangeability and that spares will fit without adjustment.

(b) Each part of which a stock will be required by the D. of E. is to be such that it may be replaced in the aircraft by a stock part without alteration to the latter being necessary. Such parts are listed with D. of E. stores Reference in the Schedule of Spare Parts. A set of master parts will be held by the Air Ministry as standards for interchangeability.

3. Special Requirements.

(a) The following requirements are to be fulfilled to the satisfaction of the D.T.D:-

(i)   A Merlin Mark I Engine is to be installed.

(ii)   The undercarriage tyres are to be suitable for an all-up weight of not less than 6,200 lb. at a tyre inflation pressure not greater than 45 lb. per sq. in.

(iii)   The attachment of the engine cowling is to be improved to obviate cracking of the panels.

(iv)   Exhaust manifolds are to be fitted.

(v)   Night flying electrical equipment is to be installed.

(vi)   The tail wheel shall be of the electrically conducting type.

(vii)   Special attention is to be given to the anti-corrosion measures.

(viii) Stowage is to be provided for two forced landing parachute flares with arrangements for their release by the pilot.

(ix)   The new flying instrument panel is to be fitted.

(x)   The R.A.E. Reflector floodlight system of instrument lighting is to be installed.

(xi)   A locker 14" × 10" × 4" (minimum) is to be provided for the stowage of the pilot's cap etc.

(xii)   The joint between the elevators is to be such that any elevator may be used with any other elevator of opposite "hand".

(xiii) At a stage in the contract, to be agreed later, the metal covered wings are to be provided instead of the fabric covered wings.

(xiv) Two R.A.E. type G. landing lamps are to be installed.

(xv)   Indicators are to be provided to show the pilot when only 50 rounds remain in each ammunition box of any two of the guns.

The following requirements will be interpreted, in the light of further experiments with the prototype aircraft K.5083.

(xvi)   The fuel system is to be modified as necessary to ensure a satisfactory supply of fuel to the engine in all operational conditions of flight whilst there is fuel remaining in the tanks.

(xvii) The cockpit sliding roof is to be made operable at all speeds.

(xviii) Adequate ventilation of the cockpit is to be provided to avoid discomfort when flying in sunshine above clouds.

(xix) The elevator trimming flap control circuit is to be improved to meet the requirements of Aircraft Design Memorandum No. 330.

(b) Should it be found necessary to alter or add to the requirements stated above, the Contractor will be notified accordingly by the Director of Contracts: modifications other than those ensuing from the present requirements may not be incorporated without written authority from the Director of Contracts. Should the present requirements or any amendment thereof result in modification whereby any part of the aircraft structure is strengthened or replaced by a stronger but otherwise interchangeable part, the contractor shall forward to the Director of Contracts as soon as possible after the inception of the modifications a statement giving the following particulars:-

(i) A description of the modifications and the parts affected thereby.

(ii) A list of the aircraft delivered prior to the issue of this specification or of amendments to the specification, i.e., the list is to include not only aircraft built in accordance with this specification but also any of the same basic type (other than experimental aircraft) built in accordance with an earlier specification in which the unmodified parts have been incorporated.

(iii) A list of those aircraft still to be delivered in which it will not be possible to incorporate the modifications.

If stocks of the unmodified parts have been supplied it shall be so stated, together with the number(s) of the contract(s) under which the supply has been made.

The expression "any part of the aircraft structure" shall be understood to mean any part (whether a single part, such as a strut or a compound part, such as a mainplane) that contributes to the strength or safety of the aircraft in flight.

4. Equipment.

(a) Equipment is to be fitted or provided for in accordance with Appendix "A" No. 808.

(b) When delivering the first aircraft and the last aircraft off each contract to which this Specification is applicable, the Contractor shall supply to the Directorate of Technical Development a copy of the relevant Appendix "A", in conformity with the current master schedule, showing the equipment then fitted to the aircraft; alternatively the Contractor shall certify to the Director of Technical Development the correctness of these appendices.

5. Inspection.

(a) For the purpose of inspection of any airframe built to this specification the aircraft shall be completely erected, and an engine with exhaust system, etc., is to be fitted therein and connected up to the pipe lines so that the fuel, oil and engine-cooling systems can be tested.

(b) The Contractor shall make such arrangements as may be necessary to show that the equipment is fitted correctly and that the wiring, piping, etc., is satisfactory as regards run and length.

6. Normal Load.

The normal load to be carried shall consist of:-

(i) The items detailed hereunder together with all parts which the Contractor must supply and fit in order that these items may be carried:-

	lb.
Pilot and parachute	200
8 Browning guns	164
2400 rounds of .303 ammunition	156
Pyrotechnics	6.5
Forced landing flares	26
Electrical equipment	1
Navigational equipment	0.5
Oxygen	14.5
First aid outfit	3
Wireless, T.R. 9(B)	52
Total	623.5

(ii) The fuel for an endurance of ¼ hour at maximum power, at sea level + 1 ¼ hours at the maximum power at which the engine can be run continuously at an altitude of 15,000 feet and oil for endurance 2 hours greater than that stated for the fuel.

7. Structural Strength.

(a) The strength of the aeroplane when flying in the fully-loaded condition shall be not less than is defined by the ultimate factors stated hereunder:-

1. Factor with the centre of pressure in its most forward position in normal flight 10

2. Factor with the centre of pressure in its most backward position in horizontal (normal) flight 7.5

3. Factor in a dive to an indicated air speed of 450 m.p.h. with the aeroplane in the terminal velocity attitude 2.0

4. Factor in a down gust of 25 f.p.s. (normal to the flight path) when the aeroplane is in an accelerated dive at the terminal velocity attitude at 1.5 times its maximum level speed 1.5

5. Factor in an up gust of 25 f.p.s. under the conditions stated at item 3 ...... 1.5

6. Factor at the angle of incidence corresponding to an inverted stall with the centre of pressure at 0.33 of the chord 5.0

(b) The aeroplane, fully-loaded, shall be able to withstand an impact with the ground at a vertical velocity of 10 feet per second, and at this velocity the impact load on the undercarriage is not to exceed three times the weight of the aeroplane, fully-loaded. The ultimate factors when the aeroplane is at rest on the ground shall not be less than the following:-

For the undercarriage 4.4

For the remainder of the aeroplane 5.0

(c) The torsional and flexural stiffnesses of the wings shall be satisfactory under the worst conditions likely to be encountered, and their natural frequencies of vibration shall be such that the lowest probable flutter speed will be above the maximum diving speed of the aeroplane or a lower speed to be agreed by the D.T.D. In calculating stiffnesses the contribution from fabric covering is to be disregarded. The Contractor shall provide facilities at his works for stiffness measurements to be made.

(d) The detailed requirements (where appropriate) of Air Publication No. 970 (May 1935) are to be satisfied and also those of all relevant aircraft design memoranda including the following – Nos. 304, 305, 312, 313, 315, 316, 318, 320, 321 and 322.

8. Final Examination.

(a) The Contractor shall provide facilities at his works for a final examination of the first aircraft of the contract in its completed, or nearly completed, state to be made on behalf of the Director of Technical Development in order that it may be seen:-

    (i)   Whether the aircraft satisfies the requirements of the Director of Technical Development in respect of its construction and equipment, or

    (ii)   Whether any alterations will be necessary prior to its delivery.

This examination shall take place as soon as possible after the aircraft has passed the final inspection required by the Director of Aeronautical Inspection.

(b) The aircraft is to be presented for examination equipped in accordance with the relevant Appendix "A". If so required, the contractor shall subsequently take out the removable equipment forming part of the military load and shall install the alternative items of removable equipment that are detailed in the Appendix "A", or he shall demonstrate that these alternative items can be installed in a satisfactory manner.

(c) The requirements referred to in clause 8(a) shall be deemed to consist of:-

    (i)   Those stated in this Specification, and

    (ii)   All supplementary and/or amended requirements (if any) of which the Contractor is given separate notice by the Director of Contracts prior to the final examination.

(d) Items of non-standard ancillary equipment which the Contractor has to supply with the aircraft are to be available for examination at the final examination of the aircraft and, if so required, the Contractor shall demonstrate their use.

(e) The Contractor will be notified by the Director of Contracts of all alterations required to be made to the air-craft and ancillary equipment consequent upon the final examination, and shall complete these alterations to the satisfaction of the Director of Technical Development.

9. Acceptance Tests.

Prior to the delivery of the first aeroplane it shall have been certified to the D.T.D. by the contractor that:-

    (i)   The aeroplane has been subjected by the Contractor's pilot to the following tests:-

        1. General flying trials in accordance with Aircraft Design Memorandum No. 291.

        2. Diving tests in accordance with Aircraft Design Memorandum No. 292.

        3. Lateral stability tests in accordance with Aircraft Design Memorandum No. 293.

4. Spinning tests in accordance with Aircraft Design Memorandum No. 294. Part I, Section 2.

5. Aerobatic flying tests in accordance with Aircraft Design Memorandum No. 295.

(ii) the above-mentioned tests have shown that the aeroplane is safe to be flown by Royal Air Force pilots.

Subsequent aeroplanes shall be tested in accordance with the requirements of A.M. Form 838 for Development and production aircraft.

10. Stability and Control.

(a) The general requirements are that the aeroplane, when fully-loaded, should:-

(i)   have positive stability about all axes;

(ii) respond quickly to the controls and be fully controllable at any speed, especially near the stall and during a steep dive, when it should have no tendency to hunt;

(iii) be easy to manoeuvre;

(iv) not be tiring to fly;

(v)   form a steady platform for firing at any speed within its range;

(vi) not experience excessive fluctuations in the speed for which it is trimmed if the throttle control is moved from the correct position for that speed to either of its limiting positions.

The aeroplane is to satisfy these requirements as completely as possible when carrying any permissible load.

(b) Effective longitudinal control is to be available at all speeds from the limiting speed to below the stalling speed.

11. Weight and Centre of Gravity.

(a) The contractor shall furnish to the Director of Technical Development or his representative (at least one week before the aircraft will be delivered) the following particulars of the 1st, 25th and last aircraft in the first batch of 50, and the last in each subsequent batch of 50, and any others which the D.T.D. may indicate:-

(1) The tare weight.

(2) The weight when fully loaded and the co-ordinates of the centre of gravity measured in the plane of symmetry from the datum point parallel and perpendicular to the datum line (see A.D.M.205).

(b) The tare weight is the weight of the aircraft when fitted with all the "Fixed" equipment, the weights of which are detailed in column 10 of the Appendix "A", with none of the removable equipment and with fuel and oil tanks empty.

(c) If the aircraft is to be delivered incompletely equipped, the particulars of the weight and centre of gravity positions are to be supplied for the aircraft with the engine installed, with the full service fuel and oil load and as completely equipped as possible.

(d) The co-ordinate of the centre of gravity parallel to the datum line is to be accurate to within 1% of the mean chord dimension. The co-ordinate of the centre of gravity perpendicular to the datum line is to be accurate to within 5% of the mean chord dimension.

(e) The centre of gravity datum point shall be marked on the aircraft in accordance with Aircraft Design memorandum No. 205.

(f) On or before completing the last aircraft off the contract the contractor shall forward to the Director of Technical Development (R.D.A.3) and analysis of the weights of its constituent parts, etc. A form suitable for the analysis will be issued to the contractor at or about the date when the contract is placed.

12. Drawings, Etc. To Be Supplied.

(a) One week before the delivery of the first aircraft built to this specification the contractor is to submit to the R.T.O. for acceptance the "Type Record" (i.e. a detailed description of the aircraft and such drawings, strength data and detailed weight data as may be required) or amendments to the Type Record, whichever is requisite.

(b) When the aircraft is handed over for type trials copies of the General Arrangement drawings of the completed aircraft shall be forwarded, with General Arrangement drawings showing the lay-out of the whole of the equipment, to the D.T.D. (R.D.A.4) in duplicate, and similarly for any subsequent aircraft, if different from the first.

(c) The D.I.S. shall be prepared as soon as possible; all relevant drawings and schedules shall be available to the Resident Technical Officer for signature prior to the delivery of the thirtieth aircraft built to this specification. Attention is drawn to the requirements relating to alteration procedure given in A.D.I.310.

TESTS TO BE MADE TO DETERMINE THE OPERATIONAL CHARACTERISTICS OF HURRICANE AIRCRAFT.

From:- 111 (Fighter) Squadron, R.A.F. Northolt.

To:- Station Headquarters, Northolt. (Copy to F/Lt. BULMAN for information. Delivered by hand.)

Date:- 21st February 1938.

Ref:- 1113/93/Air.

Further to my letter 1113/93/Air dated 14th January 1938, the following additional characteristics of the Hurricane Aircraft are forwarded for information.

Flying Characteristics.

These reports are not yet complete and further information will be forwarded as soon as experience is gained.

There is no alteration to the remarks in the original Report.

Instructions have been received that officer Commanding 111 (F) Squadron must carry out aerobatic Tests in the Hurricane and these have been done from time to time.

The Hurricane performs all aerobatics in a normal manner. A loop being started at an indicated air speed of 250 miles per hour at 5,000 feet. At a slower speed than this the aircraft stalls in an inverted position and half rolls right way up.

The slow roll is commenced at an indicated air speed of 200 miles per hour at 5,000 feet and the aircraft rolls accurately in either direction.

The roll off the loop is started at an indicated air speed of 260 miles per hour at 5,000 feet and the behaviour of the aircraft is normal.

NOTES. (1) It is anticipated that inexperienced pilots may take considerable height to recover from any mistakes they may make in aerobatics, and it is recommended that aerobatics should not be commenced below a height of 5,000 feet from the ground or when this is obscured a height of 5,000 feet from the top of the cloud layer.

(2) At the speeds required to perform these aerobatics the aircraft approaches other aircraft very rapidly and it is considered that aerobatics should not be done in conditions of bad visibility.

(3) With the speed and weight of this aircraft it is more essential than ever that control should be treated in a delicate manner.

(4) At these speeds there was no tendency for the pilot of the aircraft to "black out".

When travelling at speed these aircraft reset considerably to very bumpy weather conditions and in this unit pilots slow their aircraft down to a speed below 150 miles per hour when flying under these conditions.

2. (ii), (iii), (iv), (vi), (vii) and (viii).

No furher remarks, but information will be forwarded as it becomes available.

(v) As more pilots have now had experience of night flying the remarks contained in the original report are confirmed.

Tests have now been made to determine the efficiency of the landing lamp. These tests included taking-off and landing on an aerodrome completely dark except for the neon Beacon situated on the top of one hangar. It was found that the beam of the landing lamp as at present fitted exactly cut the exhaust flame which might cause difficulties to an inexperienced pilot. These lamps have now been trained further outboard and a fuller report embracing the views of all the pilots in the Squadron will be forwarded when all pilots in the unit have operated from a completely dark aerodrome.

In view of the fact that all pilots in this unit land looking over the left hand side, and it is thought this is true of the majority of pilots in the Royal Air Force, it is recommended that the starboard landing lamp be dispensed with and the space so made available used for installing a cine gun. If the starboard light has been fitted as a safety measure in the event of the port light filament failing it is recommended that the port light should be modified to have two filament lamps as originally used in the Royal Air Force.

3. Tests are still being carried out with regard to (a), (b), (c), (d), (e), (f), (g), (h) and (j).

Operational Characteristics.

A test for endurance was carried out at 17,000 feet at the maximum permissible boost of 4 ½ lbs. on the 10th February 1938 and 72 gallons of petrol were used in 43 minutes, giving the aircraft an endurance of 56 minutes at maximum permissible power.

(k). R/T PERFORMANCE FROM A SERVICE POINT OF VIEW.

The Hurricane has proved a particular good aircraft from the R/T point of view and considerably better results are being obtained than have ever been obtained with the Gauntlet. Though some of this improvement may be due to the great enthusiasm for R/T. within this particular Unit it is also thought that much of the improvement is due to the low noise level within the cockpit, the efficiency of the serial and the installation of the set itself.

Attached to this report are some typical range figures from which it may be seen that the range from air to ground and ground to air is likely to be at least 100 miles at operational heights though this will be confirmed by further tests.

It is emphasised that the aircraft can hear the ground station long after the ground station can hear aircraft.

Maintenance.

(a) No difficulty has been experienced in maintenance in flights though it is found that for efficient working of aircraft parts extreme cleanliness is essential and this takes considerable time.

A daily inspection takes 1 ½ hours, a 10 hour inspection 1 ½ days and a 20 hour inspection 2 days. The time for a 40 hour inspection will be forwarded when aircraft complete 40 hours.

(b) Small rings are available in lockers behind Pilots's head for screwing into either wing tip and an aircraft is tied up firmly by screw pickets in the normal manner. The control column and rudder bar are held firmly by a neat telescopic tripod arrangement and it is thought that the facilities for pegging down aircraft are very good.

(Sgnd) J . W . Gillan.
Squadron Leader, Commanding,
111 (F) Squadron, R.A.F.
NORTHOLT.

DATE.	AIRCRAFT NO.	HEIGHT.	RANGE.	REMARKS.
17.1.38	L.1551.	15,000.	2 way communication 205 miles.	This aircraft could hear Ferrett at a range of 300 miles.
17.1.38.	L.1553.	17,000	2 way range 200 miles.	2 way communication.
19.1.38.	L.1549.	5,000	North 65 miles, South 65 miles, East 95 miles West 80 miles.	" " " " " " " " " " " "
31.1.38.	L.1554 L.1553. L.1551.	1,500	40 miles Northerly	" " "
11.2.38.	L.1557.	10,000	180 miles Northerly	" " "
19.2.38.	L.1554 L.1553.	1,500	55 miles.	Ground to Air only.

CHAPTER II
Pilot Notes

A.P.1564A. Vol.I and P.N.

Revised, April, 1941
Issued with A.L. No.26

INTRODUCTION

1. The Hurricane I is a single-seater low-wing cantilever land monoplane with a retractable undercarriage and enclosed cockpit; it is powered by a Merlin II or III engine driving a Rotol or de Havilland constant-speed airscrew. The main dimensions of the aeroplane are: span 40ft., length 31 ft. 6 in. approximately.

2. The cockpit is heated indirectly from the radiator circuit and is totally enclosed under a transparent hood which slides towards the rear for purpose of entry and exit. The pilot's seat is adjustable vertically, and in some aeroplanes the occupant is protected by armour plating against attack from the front and rear. An emergency exit panel is provided in the starboard side of the decking and a knockout panel is incorporated in the sliding hood at its port front bottom corner to provide a clear view when landing should the windscreen be covered with ice. Flying controls are of the conventional stick type with a rudder bar which is adjustable horizontally for leg reach.

3. The fuselage structure consists of four tubular steel longerons, side panels of steel and duralumin tubes, and plan and bulkhead bracing of tubes and swaged wires, the tubular members being rolled to rectangular section in the vicinity of the joints. The engine and front fuselage are covered with duralumin panels, the decking with fabric-covered plywood, and the rear fuselage with fabric-covered wooden formers and stringers.

4. The cantilever main-plane, of metal construction, is built in three sections, comprising port and starboard outer planes and centre section, the last-named being integral with the fuselage. The centre section is metal covered, the two spars and four girder ribs being braced to form a rigid structure. The outer planes may be of either the fabric-covered or of the stressed-skin type; the two types are interchangeable. The fabric-covered

ailerons are mass-balanced and have a differential action. The trailing edge split-flaps are hydraulically operated and extend from the radiator fairing to the inner ends of the ailerons.

5. The cantilever tail unit components are of metal construction, with fabric covering. The fixed tail plane is attached to the top rear end of the fuselage, longitudinal trimming being obtained by trimming tabs on each horn-balanced elevator. The rudder has a small horn balance, which houses the mass balance weight, and is fitted with a balance tab operated automatically from the rudder hinge to produce a balancing action. The fin is offset to counteract engine and airscrew torque.

6. The undercarriage consists of two oleo-pneumatic shock-absorber struts which retract inwards and backwards into a well between the centre section spars, the struts being hydraulically-operated and fitted with mechanical locking, and electrical indicating devices; an audible warning device operates when the undercarriage is not locked down and the throttle is less than one-third open. Each shock-absorber strut carries a stub axle with a medium-pressure pneumatic wheel fitted with a pneumatically-operated brake controlled by a lever on the control column; differential action is provided for the brakes and operates in conjunction with the rudder bar. When on the ground, the tail is supported by a non-retractable spring-loaded shock-absorber strut which carries a fully-castoring and self-centring wheel fitted with a self-earthing tyre.

7. The main fuel tanks are housed within the centre section between the spars, one tank being fitted on each side of the fuselage, and, above the longerons, a reserve fuel tank is carried between the firewall and the instrument panel; on some aircraft, these tanks are protected by self-sealing coverings. The oil tank forms the port leading edge of the centre section. Two long-range fuel tanks can be fitted to some aircraft, one under each outer plane. A combined oil and coolant radiator is hung beneath the fuselage behind the undercarriage well and is contained in a low-velocity cowling with a flap shutter hand-operated from the cockpit.

8. Eight Browning guns, together with the necessary ammunition, are housed, four-a-side, in the outer planes and are pneumatically controlled from a single button on the control column spade grip.

9. A remotely-controlled radio-telephony transmitter-receiver is situated behind the pilot's seat and behind this instrument, a parachute flare is carried

in its launching tube on the port side. Oxygen and windscreen de-icing equipment is installed and a camera gun, operated from the control column, may be mounted on or in the leading edge of the starboard outer plane. The electrical installation provides for navigation, identification, landing, station-keeping (if fitted) and cockpit lamps, fuel gauge, engine starting, pressure head heating, wireless supply, reflector gun sight and camera gun supply. Jettison gear for the sliding hood and an upward firing device are incorporated in the fuselage.

HURRICANE I AIRCRAFT
MERLIN II OR III ENGINE

Promulgated by order of the Air Council

Air Ministry

Amended by A.L.No.48/L   A.P.1564A, Vol.I & P.N., 1.

SECTION I – CONTROLS AND EQUIPMENT

1. <u>Introduction</u>. This section gives the location of the important controls and equipment and, where necessary, explains their function and operation. The controls and equipment in the cockpit are illustrated and annotated in figs. 1 to 4, each annotated item being given an individual number; where such items are referred to in the text, the item number is quoted in brackets.

AEROPLANE CONTROLS AND EQUIPMENT

2. <u>Ailerons, elevator and rudder controls</u>. The upper portion of the control column (46), carrying the spade grip, pivots sideways about the lower portion to give aileron control; elevator control is obtained by fore-and-aft pivotal movement of the control column as a whole about its lower end. The rudder control is by a rudder bar (61) of the vertical spindle type which is adjustable for leg reach by means of a starwheel (62).

3. <u>Elevator trimming tabs control</u>. A handwheel (50), controlling the tabs, and an indicator (51), showing their position, are situated to the left of the seat; forward rotation of the handwheel corrects tail heaviness.

4. <u>Undercarriage and flap controls – general</u>. These controls are of two types, some aeroplanes being fitted with a non-automatic hydraulic system and others with an automatic system. In the non-automatic system, it is

necessary to select the desired operation of the undercarriage or flaps by means of one control and then manipulate a separate control to start the operation; in the automatic system, the function of the latter control is performed automatically.

5. <u>Undercarriage and flap controls – non-automatic system</u>. The controls consist of a selector lever and a control lever. The selector lever (66) is situated on the starboard side of the cockpit and operates in a gate with a neutral position and an UP and DOWN position for both undercarriage and flaps, the positions for operating the flaps being outboard. On early aeroplanes the knob of the lever must be pulled outwards to release the lever and enable it to be moved form an operative position, but the lever can be moved from the neutral position without first pulling out the knob. On later aeroplanes the selector lever is fitted with a catch which must be held to the lever instead of pulling out the knob. The control lever (67), which is situated outboard of the selector lever, is depressed, after the desired operation has been selected, until the operation is completed. If it is desired to lower the flaps partially, the control lever must be released immediately the flaps reach the undercarriage UP position, a safety device (65) is provided, comprising a rotating catch which obstructs the entry of the selector lever into the UP slot of the gate; the catch must be turned clockwise before moving the selector lever to the undercarriage UP position. When returning the selector lever to neutral, or to any other position, the safety catch automatically returns to the interference position.

6. If the engine-driven pump is not working, the selector lever should be left in the required position and the handpump lever (71), which is located on the starboard side of the cockpit, should be operated until the selected operation is completed; in this case the control lever need not be depressed.

7. If the handpump fails to lower the undercarriage, the selector lever should remain in the undercarriage DOWN position and the foot-operated plungers (57) and (64), painted red and situated outboard of each heel rest, should be depressed with the feet to unlock each undercarriage unit and allow them to drop under their own weight.

8. <u>Undercarriage and flap control – automatic system</u>. The method of operation of this system is the same as that of the non-automatic system except that no control lever is provided, movement of the selector lever being sufficient to effect the required operation. If it is desired to lower the flaps

partially, the selector lever must be returned to neutral immediately the flaps reach the desired position.

9. Should the engine-driven pump fail, causing loss of pressure to be shown by the pressure gauge (69) (which is provided in the automatic system only) the handpump lever (71) should be operated, with the selector lever in the required position, until the selected operation is completed.

10. If the handpump fails to lower the undercarriage the selector lever should remain in the undercarriage DOWN position and a lever, painted red and situated outboard of the port heel rest, should be pushed forward with the foot to unlock each undercarriage unit and allow them to drop under their own weight.

11. <u>Undercarriage visual indicator</u>. The "up" and "down" positions of the undercarriage units are indicated separately by red and green lamps respectively; the indicator (28) is mounted on the port side of the instrument panel and has duplicate pairs of lamps. Two switches are provided to the left of the indicator, the left-hand one (26) being the ON-OFF switch for the green lamps and the right-hand one (27), the change-over switch for the duplicate sets of lamps. The duplicate lamps are for use should it be suspected that any of the lamps normally in use have failed. A dimmer switch (29) for the lamps is mounted in the centre of the indicator. When the undercarriage is "up", the wheels are visible through two windows in the bottom of the cockpit.

12. <u>Undercarriage audible indicator</u>. Should the undercarriage units not be locked "down" at any time when the throttle lever is less than one-third open, the pilot will immediately be warned by the sounding of a buzzer (98) mounted on the port side of the cockpit.

13. <u>Flap indicator</u>. A mechanical indicator (68), showing the setting of the flaps, is situated to the right of the seat, directly below the hydraulic selector lever. The indicator pointer moves along a scale, graduated in degrees of flap movement and marked UP and Down at the extremities.

14. <u>Wheel brakes.</u> A control lever (45) for the pneumatic brakes is pivoted on the spade grip and is accessible to the pilot's right hand, the brake being operated differentially by the rudder bar for steering on the ground. A triple pressure-gauge (47), showing the air pressure in the reservoir and in each brake, is mounted forward of the foot of the control column. The brake can be locked "on" for parking by operating a retaining catch near the lever pivot;

in addition, when parking the aircraft in the open, other than for short periods in calm weather, the rudder bar should be locked in the neutral position (see para. 51) or the undercarriage wheels checked against rearward movement (ref. A.M.O.A114/38).

ENGINE CONTROLS

15. <u>Throttle and mixture controls.</u> The throttle lever (55) and the mixture lever (54) are mounted on the port upper longeron and work in slots in the cockpit decking. The mixture lever has two positions only viz. RICH and WEAK, the adjustment of the mixture strength to meet varying conditions of altitude being affected by an automatic unit on the engine. The knob of the mixture lever projects behind the throttle lever so that when the latter is moved to the CLOSED position it pushes the former to RICH position. In order to prevent movement due to vibration, the stiffness of the mixture and throttle levers can be varied by friction adjusters (52 and 53) on the inboard ends of the lever spindles; the knurled wheel adjusts the mixture lever and the serrated larger wheel, the throttle lever.

16. <u>Slow-running cut-out control.</u> The slow-running cut-out on the carburettor is operated by pulling out a knob (58) mounted under the extreme left-hand corner of the instrument panel.

17. <u>Fuel cock control.</u> On some aircraft, the fuel cock control (56) has a spring safety plate (not shown in the illustrations), which prevents the fuel supply being turned off unintentionally. The control can only be turned to the OFF position whilst the safety plate is held depressed.

18. <u>Long-range fuel tank pump switches.</u> If long-range fuel tanks are installed a switch for each pump unit is fitted on the port side of the cockpit, just above the handwheel for the elevator trimming tabs. The gauge does not register the quantity of fuel in the long-range tanks, the following method should be used when filling the main tanks from the long-range tanks. The pumps should be switched on when the main tanks contain 5 gallons and switched off immediately the contents gauge registers 25 gallons; when the contents of the main tanks are again reduced to 5 gallons the pumps should be switched on again until the main tanks contain 25 gallons, when the long-range tanks will be practically empty.

19. <u>Fuel priming pump.</u> The fuel priming pump (63) is operated by a push-and-pull actuation of the knob, the quantity of fuel injected being estimated by counting the number of strokes. The knob should be screwed on to the pump casing after use.

20. <u>Ignition switches.</u> The main ignition switches (17) controlling the two main magnetos, are on the left of the instrument panel. The starting magneto push-button (1) or booster coil push-button is on the right of the panel.

21. <u>Electric starting.</u> The electric starter push button (18), immediately to the left of the main ignition switches, controls the start of motor, the current being drawn from the aeroplane accumulator or from an external supply. A socket for the external supply, mounted on the starboard lower strut of the engine mounting, is accessible through a door in the engine cowling. A hook is fixed to the door to receive a lanyard attached to the external supply cable to relieve the socket of the weight of the cable.

22. <u>Hand starting.</u> Two starting handles are stowed in the under-carriage wheel recess beneath the centre section, one on each side wall. To remove a handle, unscrew the wing nut on the securing bracket and swing the bolt downwards; then lift the clip, disengage the starting handle and withdraw it forwards. For starting the engine, the handles are inserted through holes, one in each foremost side panel of the cowling, close to the lower end.

23. <u>Airscrew control.</u> The control lever (93) is mounted on the part side of the cockpit; a milled wheel (94) provides friction adjustment for the lever. The lever must be moved forwards to increase the engine speed and backwards to decrease the speed. In the case of de Havilland airscrews only, when the lever is fully back, the airscrew is in the "positive coarse pitch" condition.

24. <u>Radiator flap control.</u> The flap controlling the air flow through the coolant and oil radiator is adjusted by a long hand-lever (49) at the left of the seat; the lever is released for movement by pressure on a thumb-button in the top end. A mechanical indicator (48), showing the radiator flap setting, is situated on the structure tube just forward of the elevator trimming table handwheel.

25. <u>Air intake control.</u> On aeroplanes fitted with an air cleaner the temperature of the air may be varied by means of a control mounted on the port side just above the radiator shutter position indicator. When the control lever is pulled rearwards cold air passes through the filter to the intake, and when the shutter is lowered warm air enters the intake, via the filter. The control can be locked in position by means of a milled knob.

26. <u>Automatic boost control cut-out.</u> This control is situated on the left of the instrument panel. It consists of a red-painted knob (22) and must be pulled out to operate and locked by a clockwise turn. It is intended for use should the automatic boost control fail in flight or should it be necessary in an emergency to override the automatic control in order to increase the boost.

27. <u>Fuel contents gauge.</u> A single gauge (41) on the starboard side of the instrument panel indicates selectively the contents of each of the three tanks – two main and one reserve. When long-range tanks are fitted, the extra quantity of fuel is not registered by the gauge (see para.18). A switch unit, comprising a selector arm (39) and a push button (40) is mounted above the gauge. To read the contents of a tank, move the selector arm to the required position and then depress the push button. The gauge scale has upper and lower graduations, the former indicating for the reserve tank and the latter for either of the main tanks.

28. It should be noted that when the aeroplane is on the ground, the gauge readings are incorrect. A conversion table (110) showing the actual contents of the reserve and main tanks in relation to tail-down readings, is fixed to the exit panel on the starboard side of the cockpit.

28a. <u>Oil dilution valve control.</u> On certain aeroplanes, to enable easy starting under the coldest weather conditions to be made, an oil dilution valve is incorporated to inject petrol into the oil system when operated by the push button control situated at the rear of the port decking shelf. This button is to be depressed before "closing down".

OPERATIONAL EQUIPMENT

29. <u>Oxygen equipment.</u> A single oxygen cylinder is stowed below the seat. A standard regulator unit (23, 24 and 25) is mounted on the left-hand side of the instrument panel and a bayonet socket (76) for the low-pressure supply to the mask is fitted on the decking shelf alongside the port longeron. On some aircraft an additional cylinder is mounted behind the seat.

30. <u>Wireless unit controls – general.</u> A radio-telephony transmitter-receiver T.R.9B or D or T.R.1133B, is installed in the fuselage aft of the bulkhead behind the cockpit seat. Either set is switched ON from the wireless supply switch (79), mounted on the decking on the port side of the cockpit, which must be set to the OFF position at the conclusion of each flight to avoid discharging the accumulator. The remote controller which is carried on a mounting (90) on the port side of the cockpit decking above the throttle and mixture control levers, is a mechanical unit in the case of the T.R.1133B. A remote contactor and a contactor in-out switch (73) are mounted just above and on the same diagonal fuselage member as the elevator trimming tabs handwheel; the contactor may be over-ridden by setting the contactor in-out switch to OUT. (<u>Warning:</u> The contactor in-out switch should not be confused with the on-off switch on the contactor, which must not be interfered with by the pilot.) When the T.R. 1133B wireless unit is in use, the generator switch (78) must be ON; the switch is mounted on the decking on the port side of the cockpit.

The master contactor, fitted on the starboard side of the wireless bay, is provided with a heating element which must be switched off after flight by a switch adjacent to the contactor. The microphone-telephone socket is located on the electrical panel on the port side of the cockpit.

31. <u>Wireless unit mechanical controller.</u> The mechanical remote controller has a central knob and two levers, one of which projects upwards and the other downwards. The lower lever, which operates a three-position switch on the wireless unit, must be pushed forward for TRANSMIT, pulled back for RECEIVE, and moved to the vertical position to switch off the wireless unit; the lever can be locked in the OFF position by means of a latch which engages a notch in the controller casing. The upper lever operates the fine tuning control and is used during flight to make slight adjustments only, the main tuning of the receiver being pre-set on the ground. The central knob is the volume control and must be turned clockwise to increase the volume.

32. <u>Wireless unit electrical controller.</u> The electrical remote controller has a number of pushbuttons, one for switching the unit off and the others for switching the unit on and selecting pre-determined communication channels. In addition, there is a switch lever which can be moved to three positions, viz. "receive", "voice-operated" and "transmit" marked

"R", "VO", and "T", respectively. With the lever at "VO", the unit normally remains on "receive" but automatically switches to "transmit" when the pilot speaks into the microphone; if, however, the cockpit hood is open, the noise of the engine will keep the unit on "transmit" and in these circumstances the lever must be moved to "R" when reception is desired. When the guns are being used a switch, operated by the gun-firing pneumatic circuit, keeps the unit on "receive" unless the lever is moved to "T". A white lamp next to the switch lever is illuminated when the unit is receiving and goes out when the unit is transmitting. By the side of each channel-selecting button is a green lamp which is illuminated when the unit is operating on that channel.

33. Generator charge-regulator. In some aeroplanes, a generator charge-regulating switch and instruction plate regarding its use are mounted on the decking above the electrical panel. In other aeroplanes, this equipment is superseded by an automatic voltage-regulator mounted on the back of the decking bulkhead behind the cockpit seat.

34. Navigation lamps control. The navigation lamps are controlled from switch (15) which is the centre one of three switches on the left of the instrument panel, next to the main ignition switches.

35. Identification lamps controls. The identification lamps switch-box comprises a switch (100) for each lamp and a morse key (101) and provides for steady illumination or morse signalling from either lamp or from both. The switch lever for each lamp has three positions: MORSE, OFF, and STEADY, in that order from top to bottom. The spring pressure on the morse key may be altered by turning a small thumbwheel (102) at the top left-hand corner of the switchbox, the adjustment being maintained by a latch engaging one of a number of notches in the thumbwheel. The range of movement of the key may be adjusted by turning a screw in the centre of the switchbox cover after first slackening a locknut behind the cover; to enable the locknut to be reached, the cover is hinged at its left-hand edge.

36. Landing lamps controls. A two-way switch (99) on the decking shelf at the extreme left-hand corner of the instrument panel enables either the port or the starboard landing lamp to be used as required; both lamps are off when the switch is upright. A dipping control lever (74) is situated on the port side of the cockpit just aft of the engine control levers; the lamps are dipped by pushing the lever forward. The lever can be held in any position by tightening

a knurled wheel (75); when the knurled wheel is unscrewed, the lever is pulled aft into UP position by a return spring in each of the lamp units.

37. Station-keeping lamps control. On certain aeroplanes station keeping lamps are mounted, one in each side of the fuselage, so as to direct a beam of light along the trailing edges of the main plane. The ON-OFF switch (81) for the lamps is on the decking shelf on the port side of the cockpit.

38. Parachute flare release control. The control handle for releasing the parachute flare is on the starboard side of the cockpit, located out-board of, and below, the hydraulic selector lever. The handle must be pulled upwards to release the flare.

39. Gun firing controls. The guns are fired by a pneumatic circuit controlled by a pushbutton (44) fitted in the spade grip and accessible to the thumb of the left hand. The air supply is taken from the same reservoir cylinder as the brake supply, the available pressure being shown by the gauge referred to in para. 14. A milled sleeve, surrounding the pushbutton, can be rotated to a position in which it prevents operation of the button. The SAFE and FIRE positions are engraved on the sleeve and can also be identified by touch since the end of the sleeve has an identification which is at the bottom when the sleeve is in the SAFE position and comes to the side when the sleeve is turned to the FIRE position.

40. Camera gun controls. Provision is made in the gun-firing pneumatic circuit for connecting either a G.22A or B camera or a pneumatically-operated electrical switch for making exposures on G.42B cine-camera. Exposures are made by pressing either the gun-firing button (44) or the switch (not illustrated) mounted at the bottom left-hand side of the spade grip. If it is required to operate the guns and the camera simultaneously the gun-firing button should be used, but the camera only may be operated by depressing the switch. A single exposure is made with a G.22 camera each time the button is pressed; with either of the cine-cameras, a succession of exposures is made during the whole period the button is depressed.

41. When a G.22 camera is fitted, the film is advanced, the shutter re-set, and an exposure counter operated, by means of a loading handle mounted on the starboard upper longeron; the handle must be pulled out to its full extent and pushed in again. The exposure counter is mounted on the loading handle casing.

42. In conjunction with the G.42B cine-camera, a footage indicator and an aperture switch are mounted on the port side of the cockpit; the switch enables either of two camera aperture to be selected, the smaller aperture being used

in sunny weather. A stowage clip (91) is provided to receive the cable when an indicator and switch are not fitted. A main ON-OFF switch (14) for the camera gun electrical circuits is mounted on the instrument panel; it is the right-hand switch of the group of three situated immediately to the left of the instrument-flying panel.

SEATING AND EXITS

43. <u>Seat control</u>. The seat is adjustable for height by movement of a long lever (43) on the right-hand side of the seat. The seat locking device is released by pressing a thumb-button in the end of the lever.

44. <u>Safety harness locking control</u>. A control lever (113) is provided on the starboard longeron for releasing and locking the safety harness shoulder straps; the lever must be moved up to release the straps. To re-lock the straps the pilot should lean fully back before operating the lever.

45. <u>Cockpit hood locking control</u>. The cockpit hood slides fore and aft and can be locked in the fully open position by means of a control lever (77) on the port longeron just aft of the engine controls. The hood is unlocked for closing when the control lever is down, but it can be opened even if the lever is in the "locked" position.

46. <u>Break-out panel</u>. To give the pilot a clear view when landing with the windscreen covered with ice, a break-out panel is incorporated in the sliding hood at its port front bottom corner. The panel is jettisoned by pushing forward a sliding plate on the top edge of the panel, by means of a handle at its front end, and then punching out the panel into the airstream by means of the elbow.

47. <u>Emergency exit</u>. There are three methods of effecting an emergency exit from the cockpit; firstly by removing the emergency exit panel, secondly by jettisoning the cockpit hood, and thirdly by utilizing the crowbar provided.

(a) <u>Emergency exit panel</u>. A large detachable panel on the starboard side, dowelled at the bottom of the decking shelf, is held at the top by spring-loaded plungers controlled by a lever (108) on the inside of the panel. The rear top corner is also held by a bolt operated by the cockpit hood. To release the panel, the hood must be moved to its fully open position to withdraw the bolt and the lever must then be moved backward and upwards to withdraw the plungers.

(b) Jettison gear for the cockpit hood. The control lever for the jettison gear is situated on the port strut EH. To jettison the hood, pull this lever sharply in a forward and upward direction to break the wire locking the lever to the bracket, the hood will then be carried into the airstream leaving the aeroplane on the starboard side. If, however, the hood does not readily leave the aeroplane, it should be assisted by pushing it upwards, or failing that, by releasing the emergency exit panel, in addition to the jettison gear.

NOTE: When carrying out this operation it is advisable to position oneself as low as possible in the cockpit, either by lowering the seat or by adopting a crouching attitude, to avoid personal injury caused by the port side of the hood passing through the cockpit space when tearing away from the cockpit.

(c) Crowbar. A crowbar is provided to enable the pilot to extricate himself from the cockpit should the aeroplane have crashed or become damaged and the above methods prove inoperative. The crowbar is stowed in two clips attached to the starboard strut EF.

MISCELLANEOUS EQUIPMENT

48. First-aid outfit. This is attached by means of elastic cords to the inside of a detachable fairing panel on the port side, aft of the cockpit. In case of emergency the panel must be kicked in, breaking the stringers and tearing the fabric. The position of the outfit is clearly indicated on the fuselage covering.

49. Navigation equipment. A metal case (107) for maps, books, etc. is fixed to the forward end of the exit panel on the starboard side of the cockpit and a canvas case (106) for a course and height indicator is fixed to the face of the map case. A canvas case (109) for a height and airspeed computer is mounted on the exit panel, aft of the map case.

50. Fuel and oil systems diagram. A diagram (111) of the fuel and oil systems is fixed to the exit panel below the fuel contents gauge conversion table.

51. Flying controls locking gear. This gear is kept in a canvas bag which, in aeroplanes fitted with rear armour plating, is clipped to a fuselage strut in the starboard side of the wireless bay; in aeroplanes not fitted with rear armour plating, the gear is stowed in a locker behind the pilot's head. The locking gear comprises a hinged bracket for the attachment to the control column, a pair of tubes for locking the rudder bar to the bracket, and a telescopic interference tube connected to the bracket and adapted to be

passed through a slot in the back of the seat. To lock the controls, the bracket should be clamped round the top of the lower portion of the column with its projecting lugs embracing aileron actuating tie-rods and in contact with the tie-rod fork-ends nuts; movement of the hinged upper portion of the column, and hence the ailerons, is thereby prevented. The rudder bar locking tubes, which are pinned to the bracket, have quick-attachment ends for the connection to the spigot bolts clipped to the rudder bar. The interference tube prevents occupation of the seat whilst the controls are locked.

52. <u>Picketing rings</u>. A pair of picketing rings, stowed in a pocket of the flying controls locking gear bag, are provided for the attachment to screwed sockets in the undersurface of the wing spars just inboard of the wing tips.

53. <u>Weatherproof covers</u>. A weatherproof cover for the cockpit hood is stowed in the starboard side of the wireless bay in aeroplanes fitted with rear armour plating or in the locker behind the pilot's head if rear armour plating is not fitted. Two pairs of tapes, attached to the cover, tie under the fuselage to hold the cover in position, one pair passing behind, and the other pair in front of, the main plane. Covers are supplied for the airscrew blades and for the engine and air intake; they can be stowed in the wireless bay or, when guns are not installed, in the gun compartments.

54. <u>Desert equipment</u>. Certain aeroplanes are provided with desert equipment, which is stowed in the fuselage, aft of the wireless unit. A tray, mounted between port and starboard side struts, contains the following items: flying and emergency rations; drinking water tank and water bottle; screwdriver, adjustable spanner and pair of pliers; five signalling strips; and a mirror. A signal pistol is stowed on the fuselage strut at the starboard rear corner of the tray and a container for six cartridges is mounted above the pistol.

55. <u>Exhaust glare shields</u>. To prevent the pilot from being dazzled by glare from the exhausts when flying at night, shields can be fitted to the port and starboard sides of the tank cowl.

56. <u>Windscreen de-icing</u>. De-icing fluid may be fed to the windscreen by means of handpump mounted on the starboard strut, adjacent to the flap position indicator. The pump may be either of Ki-gass or Rotax design. The Ki-gass pump has a fixed delivery; the knob must be unscrewed

for use and screwed down again after use. The Rotax pump delivers its charge of fluid on the spring-energized return stroke, after the handle has been released by operation of a catch to permit the return stroke to take place. The delivery rate may be regulated by means of a knurled screw; with the screw turned fully anti-clockwise the charge is delivered in 40 sec. approximately and, with it turned fully clockwise, in 5 mins. approximately.

57. <u>Port fires</u>. A bag for stowing two port fires is attached to starboard side of the front face of the decking former aft of the pilot's seat. These portfires are to be used for destroying the aeroplane by fire should circumstances necessitate such action to be taken. Directions for use will be found on the casing of the portfires.

58. <u>Upward firing recognition device control</u>. The control for operating the recognition device is routed on the port strut CF; the operation is one of pulling the handle in an upward direction which fires a flame from the discharger unit mounted in the rear fuselage near joint J. Upon release the control will return to the normal position on its own accord. On no account must it be pushed back to normal as this will cause possible damage to the cable, resulting in the control becoming inoperative.

59. <u>Heated-clothing socket</u>. A socket for the supply of current for electrically-heated gloves and boots is stowed in clips on the electrical panel.

EARLY TYPE

LATER TYPE

Key to Fig. I

1. Starting magneto switch
2. Radiator temperature gauge
3. Oil pressure gauge
4. Oil temperature gauge
5. Rate-of-climb indicator
6. Turning indicator
7. Artificial horizon
8. Direction indicator
9. Adjusting knob for (8)
10. Altimeter
11. Zero-adjusting knob for (10)
12. Air-speed indicator
13. Clock
14. Cine-camera switch
15. Navigation lamps switch
16. Pressure-head heater switch
17. Main magnetos switches
18. Electric starter push-button
19. Chronograph knob for (13)
20. Arrester knob for (13)
21. Winding and setting knob for (13)
22. Automatic boost cut-out control
23. Oxygen regulator control valve
24. Oxygen delivery indicator
25. Oxygen supply indicator
26. ON-OFF switch for (28)
27. Change-over switch for (28)
28. Undercarriage position visual indicator
29. Dimmer switch for (28)
30. Compass correction card holder
31. Control knob for (32)
32. Reflector sight dimming screen
33. Crash pad
34. Spare lamps stowage for reflector sight
35. Engine-speed indicator
36. Socket for plug from reflector sight

37. ON-OFF switch for reflector sight
38. Dimmer switch for reflector sight
39. Boost pressure gauge
40. Fuel contents gauge selector push-button
41. Fuel contents gauge
42. Fuel pressure gauge

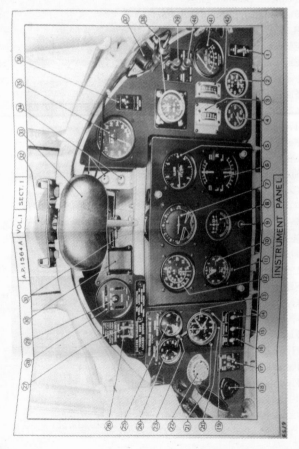

Fig. 1

Key to Fig. 2

43 Seat height-adjusting lever
44 Gun firing button
45 Brakes control lever
46 Control column
47 Triple air-pressure gauge
48 Radiator flap position indicator
49 Radiator flap control lever
50 Elevator trimming tabs control handwheel
51 Elevator trimming tabs control indicator
52 Friction adjuster for (54)
53 Friction adjuster for (55)
54 Mixture control lever
55 Throttle control lever
56 Fuel cock control
57 Undercarriage EMERGENCY release – port
58 Slow-running cut-out control
59 Cockpit floodlamp
60 Compass
61 Rudder bar
62 Rudder bar adjusting starwheel
63 Fuel priming pump
64 Undercarriage EMERGENCY release – starboard
65 Safety catch for (66)
66 Hydraulic selector lever
67 Hydraulic control lever
68 Flaps position indicator
69 Hydraulic pressure gauge
70 Parachute flares releases
71 Hydraulic handpump operating lever

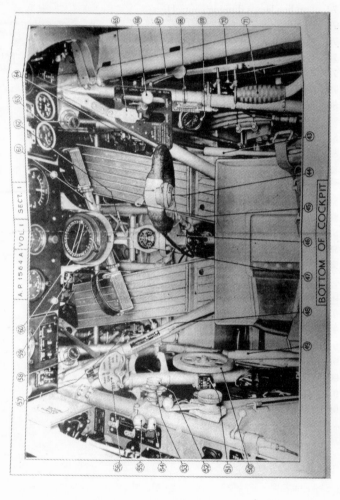

BOTTOM OF COCKPIT

Fig. 2

Key to Fig. 3

72 Socket for remote contactor cable
73 Contactor "IN-OUT" switch and mounting bracket
74 Landing lamps dipping control lever
75 Friction adjuster for (74)
76 Oxygen bayonet socket
77 Cockpit hood locking control
78 Generator switch
79 Wireless supply switch (for T.R. 9D or T.R. 1133)
80 Microphone-telephone socket
81 Formation-keeping lamps switch
82 Ammeter
83 Voltmeter
84 Clips for T.R.1133 controller cable
85 Socket for T.R. 9B or D volume controller cable
86 Cockpit floodlamp
87 Stowage for T.R. 1133 controller cable
88 Dimmer switch for (86)
89 Engine data plate
90 Mounting for wireless unit controller
91 Stowage for cine-camera footage-indicator cable
92 Mounting for cine-camera footage-indicator
93 Airscrew control lever
94 Friction adjuster for (93)
95 Cockpit floodlamp
96 Dimmer switch for (95)
97 Dimmer switch for (59)
98 Undercarriage position audible indicator
99 Landing lamps switch

A.P. 1564 A | VOL. I | SECT. I

PORT SIDE OF COCKPIT

Fig. 3

Key to Fig. 4

100 Identification lamps switches
101 Identification lamps morse key
102 Spring pressure control for (101)
103 Cockpit floodlamp
104 Dimmer switch for (103)
105 Position of loading handle for G.22A or B camera
106 Course and height indicator case
107 Map case
108 EMERGENCY exit panel control lever
109 Height and airspeed computer case
110 Fuel contents gauge conversion table
111 Fuel and oil systems diagram
112 Cockpit hood handle
113 Safety harness locking control
114 Locker door – shown open (inaccessible when rear armour plating
    is fitted)

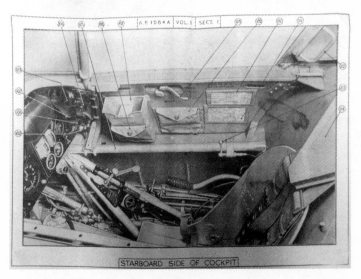

STARBOARD SIDE OF COCKPIT

Fig. 4

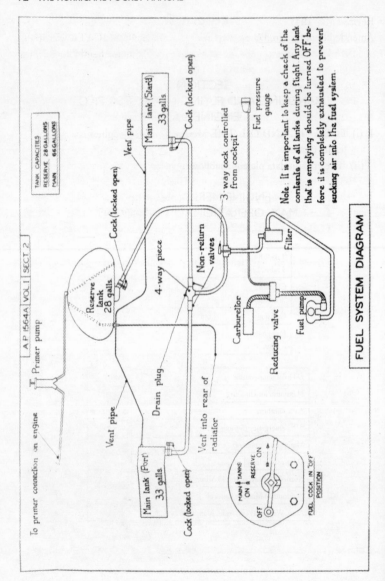

FUEL SYSTEM DIAGRAM

Revised May 1941
Amended by A. L. No.37

AIR PUBLICATION 1564 A
Volume I and Pilot's Notes

SECTION 2
HANDLING AND FLYING NOTES FOR PILOT
ENGINE DATA

1. (i) FOR FUEL AND OIL THE Merlin II and III engines see A.P.1464, leaflet C.37.

  (ii) The cockpit data plate is as follows:-

ENGINE MERLIN II (OR III)
MAX. OPERATIONAL LIMITATIONS

	R.P.M.	Boost lb./sq.in
Take-off 3 mins. Limit	3,000	+6¼
Climbing ½ hr. limit	2,600	+6¼
Cruising	2,600	+4½
Emergency 5 mins. limit	3,000	+6¼

Oil inlet temperature	°C.
Maximum for climbing	90
" " climbing	90
" " emergency (5 mins.)	95
Minimum for take-off	15
Oil pressure lb. sq.in.	
Normal 60 Emergency 45 Minm. (5 mins.)	
Economical Mixture Control	
Auto. Weak + 2¼ lb. sq.in. Maximum boost	

(iii) <u>The following limitations should also be noted</u>:-

Take-off	Minimum r.p.m. 2,080
Diving	Maximum boost + 6¼ lb/sq.in Maximum r.p.m. 3,600 3,000 r.p.m. may be exceeded only for 20 seconds with throttle more than one-third open.
Combat concession (½ hr. limit, see Sub.para.(v) below)	Maximum r.p.m. below 20,000 ft. 2,850 Maximum r.p.m. above 20,000 ft. 3,000

Coolant Temperature:-

	°C
Minimum for take-off	60
Maximum continuous	95
Maximum for ½ hour	120

(iv) <u>Concessions when 100 octane fuel is used</u>:-

Combat	Maximum boost + 12 lb/sq.in. Obtained by operating boost Control out-out (see sub para. (v) below).
Cruising with Weak mixture	Boost may be + 2¼ lb/sq.in. Between 1,800 and 2,600 r.p.m.

(v) <u>Note re combat concessions</u>:-

The maximum combat r.p.m. and boost given in sub-paras. (iii) and (iv) above are only to be used if necessitated by operations and, if used, details must be reported upon landing to ensure that an entry is made in the engine log book.

(vi) Fuel pressure:-

Main tanks	2 to 2½ lb/sq.in.
Reserve tanks	2½ to 3 lb/sq.in.

FLYING LIMITATIONS AND SPEEDS

2. For diving:-	390 m.p.h. I.A.S.
With undercarriage down:-	120 m.p.h. I.A.S.
With flaps down:-	120 m.p.h. I.A.S.

PRELIMINARIES

3. (i) Switch on the undercarriage indicator lamps (port switch) when two green lights should show. Test the change-over switch.

(ii) See that the short (lower) arm of the safety catch for the hydraulic selector is across the WHEELS UP slot of the gate.

(iii) See that cockpit hood is locked open.

STARTING THE ENGINE

4. (i) Set:-

Throttle	- ½ in. open
Mixture control	- RICH
Airscrew speed control	- Fully back
Fuel cock	- MAIN TANKS ON
Radiator shutter	- OPEN

(ii) Operate the priming pump to prime the suction and delivery pipes. This may be judged by a sudden increase in resistance of the plunger.

(iii) Switch ON the main and starting magnetos.

(iv) Press the starting button or begin hand starting and, at the same time, operate the priming pump rapidly. The number of strokes which must be given while the engine is being turned, before it may be expected to start, is as follows:-

Air temperature °C.	+30	+20	+10	0	-10
Normal fuel:	3	4	7	13	
High volatile fuel:				3	8

The engine should start without greatly exceeding the above number of strokes, or after not more than two if the engine is hot.

(v) Turning periods should not exceed 20 seconds, with an interval of at least 30 seconds between each attempt.

(vi) At temperature below 0°C., it may be necessary to continue priming after the engine fires and until it is running satisfactorily.

(vii) As soon as the engine is running evenly switch off the starting magneto and screw down the priming pump.

(viii) If the main tanks are less than half full, take off on the reserve tank, but do not forget to change over to main tanks when at a safe height.

TESTING ENGINE AND INSTALLATIONS

5. (i) While warming up, take the usual checks of pressures, temperatures, and operation of controls and flaps.

a. Brake pressure should be at least 100 lb/sq.in.

(ii) After a few minutes move the airscrew speed control slowly fully forward.

(iii) After warming up, open throttle to give maximum boost for cruising in WEAK mixture and test the operation of the constant speed airscrew.

(iv) Open up to maximum boost for cruising in RICH mixture and test each magneto in turn. The drop in r.p.m. should not exceed 150.

(v) Open the throttle fully and check r.p.m. boost and oil pressure.

FINAL PREPARATIONS FOR TAKE-OFF - DRILL OF VITAL ACTIONS

6. "T.M.P. Fuel, Flaps and Radiator":-

    T - Trimming tabs - Neutral

    M - Mixture - RICH

    P - Pitch - Airscrew speed control fully forward.

    Fuel - Cock to MAIN TANKS ON: Check contents of tanks (see. Para. 4.(viii)).

    Flaps - UP (if taking off from a small aerodrome, the flaps may be set at 28° down – two divisions on the indicator)

    Radiator - Shutter fully OPEN.

TAKE OFF

7. (i) Any tendency to swing can be countered by coarse use of the rudder.

  (ii) After raising the undercarriage return the selector lever to neutral.

  (iii) Do not start to climb before a safe speed of 140 m.p.h. A.S.I.R. is attained.

ENGINE FAILURE DURING TAKE-OFF

8. (i) Put undercarriage selector lever in UP position and operate the hand pump if necessary.

  (ii) Turn the fuel cock to OFF and switch OFF the ignition.

  (iii) If there is time, lower the flaps.

CLIMBING

9. (i) If the take-off has been made on the reserve tank, change over to the main tanks upon reaching a safe height.

  (ii) Climb at 170 m.p.h. A.S.I.R. up to 10,000 feet, after which a reduction of 1 m.p.h. for each additional 1,000 feet should be made.

GENERAL FLYING

10. (i)   This aeroplane is stable about all axes.

   (ii)   <u>Change of trim</u>:

Flaps down -	Nose goes down
Undercarriage down -	Nose goes very slightly down.

   (iii) Greatest range is obtained by flying in WEAK mixture at about 1,700 r.p.m. and 150 m.p.h. A.S.I.R. Approximately the same range will be obtained at the same A.S.I.R. at any height. Greatest endurance is obtained at 120 m.p.h. A.S.I.R.

   (iv)   For stretching a glide in the event of a forced landing, the airscrew speed control should be pulled right back. With flaps and undercarriage up, the gliding angle is very flat at speeds of 120-140 m.p.h. A.S.I.R.

STALLING

11. (i)   At the stall one wing usually drops sharply, often over the vertical, with flaps either up or down.

   (ii)   <u>Stalling speeds:</u>
   Flaps and undercarriage up 77 m.p.h. A.S.I.R.
   Flaps and undercarriage down 63 m.p.h. A.S.I.R.

SPINNING

12. (i)   Spinning is permitted by pilots who have written permission from the C.O. of their Squadron (C.F.I. of an O.T.U.). The following height limits are to be observed:
   Spins are not to be started below 10,000 feet.
   Recovery must be started not lower than 5,000 feet.

   (ii)   Ample speed should be attained before starting to ease out of the resultant dive.

DIVING

13. (i)   Generally, set the airscrew to govern at cruising r.p.m.

   (ii)   If desired to close the throttle in a dive, pull back airscrew speed control also. With the D.H. 20° constant speed airscrew the lever must be pulled right back to the positive coarse pitch position, otherwise the airscrew may go into fine pitch and stay there, resulting in excessive r.p.m. in the dive.

After recovery from the dive, advance the airscrew speed control again before opening the throttle.

(iii) With this airscrew the pilot must watch the r.p.m. during the dive so as not to exceed the limitations given in para.1.

(iv) At high r.p.m. the throttle must be more than one third open.

(v) In a dive the aeroplane becomes tail heavy as the speed increases. The trimming tabs should be used with care. Also care should be taken not to allow the aeroplane to yaw in a dive, as this produces a marked nose-down pitching tendency.

AEROBATICS

14. Aerobatics on this aeroplane are normal and easy. Owing to its high performance, care must be taken not to impose excessive loads and not to induce a high-speed stall. Many aerobatics may be done at much less than full throttle. Cruising r.p.m. should be used, because if engine speed is reduced below this, detonation might occur if the throttle is opened up to full boost for any reason. The following speeds are recommended for aerobatics:-

(i) <u>Looping</u>.- Speed should be about 300 m.p.h. A.S.I.R. but may be reduced to 220-250 m.p.h. when the pilot is fully proficient.

(ii) <u>Rolling</u>.- Speed should be at least 250 m.p.h. A.S.I.R. the nose should be brought up about 45° above the horizon at the start, the roll being barrelled just enough to keep the engine running throughout.

(iii) <u>Half roll off loop</u>.- Speed should be at least 300 m.p.h. A.S.I.R.

(iv) <u>Upward roll</u>.- Speed should be at least 300 m.p.h. A.S.I.R.

(v) <u>Flick manoeuvres</u>.- Speed should be about 140 m.p.h. A.S.I.R., and boost pressure should be low. On no account carry out flick manoeuvres except at low speeds and allow ample height for recovery in the event of an accidental spin.

APPROACH AND LANDING

15. (i) Reduce speed to 120 m.p.h. A.S.I.R. See that the cockpit hood is locked open and carry out the Drill of Vital actions "U.M.P., and flaps".

U - Undercarriage	- DOWN (Check that green lights appear)
M - Mixture control	- RICH
P - Pitch	- Airscrew speed control fully formed.
Flaps	- DOWN

(ii) <u>Undercarriage:</u> - When lowering the undercarriage be careful to disengage the thumb catch by easing the selector lever forward before trying to move it from the UP to the DOWN position, otherwise the lever may become jammed in the UP position. Return the lever to neutral as soon as the undercarriage is down.

(iii) <u>Flaps:</u> - If 120 m.p.h. is exceeded with the flaps down, they will be partially raised by the airflow and, in the case of aeroplanes fitted with the non-automatic system, it is necessary to depress the hydraulic control lever to lower them again.

(iv) Correct speeds for the approach:-

Engine assisted	-	about	85	m.p.h. A.S.I.R.
Glide	-	"	90	" "
The Creeper	-	"	75	" "

MISLANDING

16. (i) Open the throttle fully and wait a few seconds before starting to climb.

(ii) Raise the undercarriage as soon as possible.

(iii) Climb at about 90 m.p.h. A.S.I.R.

(iv) After reaching a safe height of not less than 300 feet at a speed of not less than 120 m.p.h. A.S.I.R. raise the flaps.

LANDING ACROSS WIND

17. The aeroplane can be landed across wind but it is undesirable that such landings should be made if the wind exceeds about 20 m.p.h.

AFTER LANDING

18. (i) Before taxying in raise the flaps and open the radiator shutter.

(ii) After taxying in, set the airscrew speed control fully back and open up the engine sufficiently to change pitch to coarse.

(iii) Allow the engine to idle for a few seconds and operate the slow-running out-out and, when the engine stops, release it and turn the fuel cock to OFF and switch OFF the ignition.

(iv) Switch OFF all electrical switches and see that the safety plate of the hydraulic undercarriage selector is covering the wheels UP position.

FLYING IN BAD WEATHER

19. When visibility is extremely bad, the flange may be lowered about 40° (about 3 divisions) and the speed reduced to about 100 m.p.h. I.A.S. The radiator shutter must be opened to keep the temperature at about 100°C.

POSITION ERROR TABLE

20. The corrections for position error are as follows:-

At	80	m.p.h.	I.A.S.	Add	6	m.p.h.
"	100	"	"	"	3	"
"	120	"	"	"	0	"
"	140	"	"	Subtract	2	"
"	160	"	"	"	4	"
"	180	"	"	"	6	"
"	200	"	"	"	7	"
"	200/250	"	"	"	9	"

21. FUEL AND OIL CAPACITY AND CONSUMPTION

(i) Fuel.   Gallons

Two main tanks	33 gallons each	66
One reserve tank	-	28
Total normal capacity:		94
Two long-range tanks (if fitted)		
43 gallons each:		36
Total long range capacity:		180

(ii) Oil.

Effective capacity: 7½ to 9 gallons.

(iii) Fuel consumption.-

Max r.p.m. and boost for:	Height feet:	Consumption gallons per hour:
Climbing	12,000	81
Cruising RICH	14,500	68
" WEAK	18,500	49
Most economical cruising (1700 r.p.m. 150 m.p.h. I.A.S.)	14,000	25
All-out	17,000	89

22. ABANDONING BY PARACHUTE

When abandoning by parachute, it is important to decrease speed and then to dive over the side immediately. The pilot must not stand on the seat and delay in jumping, or he will hit either the aerial mast or the tail plane.

22A. FIRE IN THE AIR

See Note in A.P.2095, Pilot's Notes General. Fire can be caused by a serious leakage of coolant in contact with hot exhausts. Warning is given by streams of white vapour from the exhaust manifolds, when the pilot should carry out the fire drill given in A.P.2095, except that the fire extinguisher need not be operated if the fire has not started. The engine must not be restarted.

23. NOTES ON THE SEA HURRICANE

(i) <u>Increased boost:</u>

The use of lb/sq.in. Boost is permitted for periods of about 15 minutes at low altitudes. The radiator shutter should be left open when the increased boost is used and it must be remembered that the fuel consumption will be increased by nearly 60%. The temperature of the coolant and the oil may be permitted to rise to 135°C. outlet and 105°C. inlet respectively under these emergency conditions.

(ii) <u>Long range fuel tanks:</u>

    (a) Two long range fuel tanks, each of 44 gallons capacity, are fitted below the main planes, one under each wing.

    (b) Both tanks are jettisonable, the jettison lever being next to the fuel cock control on the starboard side of the cockpit.

    (c) The fuel cock control is marked OFF, PORT and STARBOARD, and the jettison lever cannot be moved until the fuel cock control is turned OFF.

(iii) <u>Management of long range fuel tanks:</u>

    (a) Take-off in the normal way on the main tanks.

    (b) After a safe height of 1,000 – 2,000 feet change over to a jettisonable tank and turn off the main fuel system.

    (c) When the jettisonable tank is empty and the engine cuts, change over to the second jettisonable tank and at the same time turn ON the reserve tank of the main fuel system. The effect is to prime the whole system from the gravity tank and the engine will pick up. When it picks up turn OFF the reserve tank and continue using the second jettisonable tank.

    (d) When this jettisonable tank is empty and the engine cuts, turn ON the main tanks. If the engine does not pick up on the main tanks, prime the system by using the reserve tank as before.

(iv) <u>Deck take-off</u>:- The drill of Vital Actions is the same as that for normal take-off but the 28° position of the flaps should be used.

(v) <u>Deck Landing</u>:-

    (a) On approaching the carrier before landing, lower the arrester hook. A green light appears on the hook release mounting when the hook has completed ⅓ of its travel.

        The lowering of hooks should preferably be done before breaking formation, where applicable, as an additional check can then be made by pilots of other aeroplanes.

    (b) Reduce speed to 95 knots I.A.S. and see that the cockpit hood is locked open.

    (c) Check brake pressure – minimum 100 lb/sq.in.

    (d) Drill of Vital Actions - "U.M.P., hook and flaps"

U	- Undercarriage	- DOWN (check green lights)
M	- Mixture	- RICH
P	- Pitch	- Propeller speed control fully forward.
Hook	- Arrester gear	- DOWN (check green lights)
Flaps -		DOWN

    (e) Approach at 65 knots I.A.S.

(vi) <u>Accelerated take-off</u>.-

    (a) This aeroplane can be catapulted or accelerated. The maximum and minimum limits of weight are given on the Loading and C.G. Diagram.

    (b) Before take-off, the pilot should see that the cockpit hood is locked open and he must have his head back against the head rest.

CHAPTER III
Tactical

SECRET   A.F.C.116

AIR FIGHTING DEVELOPMENT UNIT,
R.A.F. STATION, DUXFORD,
REPORT
No.31
on

Tactical Trials With Hurricane Aircraft Fitted To Carry Bombs
Ref:- AFDU/3/19/37
Cross Ref:- A. & A.E.E. Reports A&AEE/S.520/Arm., and AAEE/689

INTRODUCTION

1. In accordance with Headquarters, Fighter Command letter FC/S.22332/ Tactics, dated 18.6.41, trials were carried out at this Unit to determine the suitability of Hurricane fighters carrying bombs for the following purpose:-

(i)   Against armoured fighting vehicles.

(ii) Against merchant ships.

(iii) For short range intruder operations.

(iv) As a means of bringing enemy fighters to action during fighter sweeps.

2. In each case the security of the Hurricane against flak or enemy fighters has been considered and also the question of fusing for the various bombs and methods of attack.

BRIEF DESCRIPTION OF THE AIRCRAFT

3. Hurricane II, Z.3451 and Hurricane I, P.2989, were allotted to this Unit on 24.6.41 for the purpose of the trials.

4. The aircraft are capable of carrying two 250 lb. bombs on a modified universal carrier.

5. Bombing controls for the pilot consist of a fusing switch, selector switched for port and starboard, and a release button on the top of the throttle lever. All the special equipment proved entirely satisfactory.

6. The aircraft carrying out the trials can only use six guns, as the ejection chutes for two guns were removed to allow for the fitting of the bomb carriers and can reassume their normal role of fighter as soon as the bombs have been released. It is understood that a modification can be incorporated to allow the 8 guns to be retained.

7. Handling – It was found that with two 250 lb. bombs attached, the Hurricane manoeuvred normally under all conditions. No difficulties were encountered with only one bomb in position.

A Hurribomber being armed with 250lb bombs, RAF Manston,
6 November 1941.

DETAILS OF TRIALS

General

8. 11½ lb. and 250 lb. practice bombs were dropped on the BASSINGBOURN Range and on a target representing a hulk of a ship in THE WASH; marking facilities were available for the both targets. Attacks were also carried out against a moving target towed by an armoured car at about 8–10 m.p.h., across DUXFORD Aerodrome.

AGAINST ARMOURED FIGHTING VEHICLES

9. Low Level Attacks – This attack provided the best results, and also gave the Hurricane the safest method of approach, as once the target had been

sighted, a very low jinking approach could be made and the final run-up to the target left to the last moment. Releasing eight bombs at a height of 50 feet, it was found that the average error varied between 16.5 yds. and 22.4 yds. With four bombs released from 50 feet, the average error was 18.3 yds. Attacks were also made at 500 feet but the results were not quite so good.

10. The only satisfactory target for such attacks would be a concentration of heavy vehicles, into which it would be possible to drop 250 lb. G.P. Bombs with 11 seconds delay. This would not however be entirely satisfactory as during the trials it was found that on hard ground frequent ricochets occurred. Instantaneous fusing cannot be used owing to the danger to the attacking aircraft.

11. Dive Attacks – Dives were made from 3,000 feet down to 1,000 feet, releasing at about 1,500 feet and from 4,000 feet to 2,000 feet, releasing at 2,500 feet. The average error against a stationary target at the higher release height was 24 yards and at the lower release height about 27 yards. This type of attack, however, loses the advantage of surprise and renders the fighter more vulnerable to A.A. fire. It is considered that in these attacks, 250 lb. G.P. bombs with instantaneous fuses can be dropped safely providing the fighter pulls out of the dive by 1,000 feet.

12. Both dive and low level attacks were carried out against a moving target. No accurate marking was available, but the results observed appeared to be quite as good as those obtained against the stationary target. The target was moving at 8–10 m.p.h., and could take no evasion.

AGAINST MERCHANT SHIPS

13. Use of a stationary target simulating a ship was obtained, and various attacks were carried out with 11½ lb. practice bombs. The best results were obtained when attacking with the lowest approach possible on the beam of the ship at about 230–260 m.p.h., I.A.S. The bomb was released at heights up to 50 feet, when the aircraft was flying level, the object being to hit the ship near the water line, using the bomb as a form of torpedo. The Hurricane made its 'get-away' from the target either by going over the ship or turning across the stern and continuing as low and as fast as possible, at the same time jinking. This approach, besides being the most effective, renders the fighter less vulnerable than in a dive attack and allows it to achieve an element of surprise.

14. This form of attack is being used successfully by Blenheim units of No. 2 Bomber Group, carrying 250 lb. S.A.P. bombs with 11 seconds delay.

15. During the trials dive attacks were also carried out, and although reasonably good results were obtained, the fighter would be more vulnerable to A.A. fire. In such an attack a 250 lb. S.A.P. bomb with instantaneous detonator in the tail could be used.

SHORT RANGE INTRUDER OPERATIONS

16. By day in bad weather conditions it is thought that good use can be made of the bombing Hurricane with 250 lb. G.P. bombs with 11 seconds delay against buildings. The most suitable approach appears to be low level with continual jinking until the final run-up to the target.

17. If weather conditions and lack of defensive fire allow, dive bombing attacks can be carried out, in which case 250 lb. G.P. bombs with instantaneous fuse can be carried.

AS A MEANS OF BRINGING ENEMY FIGHTERS
TO ACTION DURING FIGHTER SWEEPS

18. Since there is no adequate method of sighting, high level bombing is considered impracticable and therefore accurate bombing attacks to bring enemy fighters into action would have to be either dive or low level as described above.

SIGHTING

19. Diving Attacks – The G.M.2 sight can be used to assist the pilot to make a steady dive on the target, but results just as accurate were obtained by sighting along the top of the cowlings. Exact timing for release depends upon height, wind, and angle of dive, but it was found by pilots of this Unit that very little practice was required to become proficient. The best diving angle is about 45 degrees.

20. Low Level – This can only be done by sighting along the side of the nose and again the time to release will depend on the height, speed and wind. As a rough guide, it was found that when at about 50 foot at 240 m.p.h., the target appeared a nose length ahead of the aircraft for correct release in conditions of little wind.

CONCLUSIONS

21. Good results can be obtained in low level and dive bombing attacks with very little practice.

22. For dive attacks the best approach is at an angle of about 45 degrees.

23. Low level bombing gave the most accurate results against all types of targets and should give the attacking fighter the greatest measure of security.

24. Results obtained against a moving target appeared as accurate as on the stationary ones. The target was, however, moving at only 8–10 m.p.h., and unable to take any evasion.

25. No special sight is required.

7th August 1941.

Wing Commander,
Commanding, A.F.D.U.

HURRICANE
DIVE BOMBING TRIALS
29.6.41.

8 Bombs
Released at 1,500 ft. approx.
Average 30.5 yds.

8 Bombs – 1 Direct Hit
Released at 1,500 ft. approx.
Average 26.6 yds.

4 Bombs
Released at 1,500 ft. approx.
Average 25.8 yds.

4 Bombs
Released at 2,500 ft. approx.
Average 31.5 yds.

8 Bombs
Released at 2,500 ft.
Average 20.4 yds.

8 Bombs
Released at 2,500 ft.
Average 26.0 yds.

Scale 1' to 100 yds.

HURRICANE
LOW LEVEL BOMBING TRIALS
5.7.41.

8 Bombs – 2 Direct Hits
Released up to 50 ft. alt.
Average 22.9 yds.

8 Bombs
Released up to 50 ft. alt.
Average 16.4 yds.

Target
Triangle
16 ft. sides

4 Bombs
Released up to 50 ft. alt.
Average 18.8 yds.

<u>Scale 1' to 100 yds.</u>

HURRICANE
BOMBING TRIALS
9.7.41.

Direction
of attack

Sea

Low level
8 Bombs
Released up to 50 ft. alt.

Land

Target Ship
Length - 300 ft.
Breadth at waterline - 40 ft.
Height of Mast - 95 ft.

Low Level
4 Bombs
Released up to 50 ft. alt.

Dive Attack
8 Bombs
Released at 1,500 ft. approx.

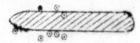

CHAPTER IV
Operations

OPERATIONS RECORD BOOK R.A.F. Form 540
   of (Unit of Formation)---------No.-----111 Squadron------ No. of pages used
for day-----

Place.	Date.	Time.	Summary of Events.	References to Appendices
Debden.	2/9/40		Nine Hurricanes 111 Squadron F/Lt Giddings, F/O Bowring P/O Ritchie F/L Bruce P/O. Simpson, Sgts Hampshire, Ekins, Dymond D.F.M. and Brown were ordered to patrol from Castle Camps at 1230 hours and to link up with 46 Squadron over Rochford at 15,000'. At 1250 hours 20 Heinkels 111's with fighter escort were sighted proceeding over the Thames Estuary in a westerly direction. The bombers were flying in vics of five. Red 1 F/Lt. Giddings led his section into a head-on attack on one big formation, and F/O. Bowring, Red 2 dived to within 50 yards of leading Heinkel getting in a three second burst and observed pieces of metal flying off his target, before being attacked by ME 110. Red 1 after his initial attack force landed at Detling, and was subjected to machine gunning, bombing, from the air after landing. Red 3 P/O. Ritchie who followed in force landed at Rochford with no damage. Yellow 2 Sgt Hampshire after observing A.A. fire to the South west turned in that direction and sighted enemy slightly below. He selected one ME 110 as his target and followed it firing a long burst which caused enemy's starboard engine to make profusely. Yellow 3 Sgt Ekins dived on a HE 111 got in a good burst causing the port engine to smoke before being attacked by an ME 109 which he fired on without any apparent result. Sgt Dymond, Yellow 1 was missing after the action and is thought to have been shot down over the Thames Estuary. F/Lt. Bruce Blue 1, saw one Heinkel 111 crash into the sea after being shot up by the squadron generally. He followed this attack by damaging an ME 110 with 2 bursts of 2 secs, but had to break away when attacked by an ME 109. P/O. Simpson, Blue 2, dived on	

			a Heinkel 111 and opened fire at 300 yards closing to 50 yards and observed enemy starboard engine idling. He was attacked by an ME 109 and broke off when he found his sliding cockpit roof and fuselage had been hit. Blue 3 Sgt Brown dived into the second vic formation and got in a good burst on a Heinkel 111 and followed with a 2 sec burst on an ME 109 which climbed for cloud cover with Glycol pouring from it. He also noticed pieces of metal fall from Heinkel he originally attacked. Summary of Losses. Our Sgt Dymond D.F.M. missing. Enemy's 1 Heinkel 111 destroyed (by Squadron) 1 Heinkel 111 probably destroyed (by Squadron) 1 Mg 110 probably destroyed Sgt Hampshire 2 ME 110 damaged (F/Lt Bruce F/O Bowring) 2 Heinkels 111 damaged (P/O. Simpson, Sgt Ekins) 1 ME 109 damaged (Sgt Brown).	
Croydon.	3/9/40		Squadron returned to Croydon from Debden.	
	4/9/40		8 Hurricanes 111 Squadron, F/Lt Giddings, F/Lt Bruce, P/O. Simpson, P/O. Maccinski, P/O. Atkinson, F/O Bowring, Sgts Wallace and Silk left Croydon for Hawkings at dawn and were ordered to patrol Folkestone 0900 hours. (Sgt Silk did not take off.) Several large formations of enemy fighters were engaged five miles east of Folkestone. Enemy aircraft were flying singly or in pairs and were stepped up to 30,000 in very loose formation. Enemy fighter formations converged on our Squadron when they engaged and appeared to surround them. Red 1 F/Lt Giddings led the attack on the enemy fighters at 21,000 and made a head-on attack. He was followed in by Red 2 F/O. Bowring and Red 3 Sgt Wallace, P/O. Simpson Green 2 followed Red 3 and the two missing officers F/Lt Bruce and P/O. Maccinski followed on. P/O Atkinson did not engage with any apparent effect, but F/Lt Giddings shot down 2 ME 109s in flames with x 4 and 5 second bursts. These two enemy planes were flying at the rear of a formation and made no apparent effort to avoid his. He also damaged one ME 109 in his first head-on attack. He force landed at Staplecross due to an attack from astern which pierced his oil pipe, but was uninjured. Sgt Wallace shot down one ME 109, the pilot baling out 5 miles east of Folkestone, during the general engagement and saw his tracers entering 3 more ME 109s. F/O Bowring who suffered slight damage and had one	

			bullet explode in his cockpit saw 1 ME 109 down in flames over the Sea, and engaged several other enemy aircraft. F/O Simpson also destroyed one ME 109 which was seen to dive into the Sea with smoke pouring from the engine. Result of the engagement:- 5 ME 109 destroyed (F/Lt Giddings 2, F/O Bowring, P/O. Simpson and Sgt Wallace) 5 damaged probably. Our Losses:- F/Lt Bruce and P/O. Maccinski missing, the latter was seen to bale out over the sea, and was shot at by enemy fighters, although both F/O Bowring and Sgt Wallace attempted to protect him as he came down.
			
			  The Following postings to the Squadron:-
			  F/O. Kustrymaki 31/8/40 from 6 O.T.U.
			  P/O. Maccinski 31/8/40 from 6 O.T.U.
			  Sgt. Bumstead. 27/8/40 from 17 Squadron.
			  Sgt Page & Porter. 31/8/40 from 6 O.T.U.	

Croydon.	5/9/40		8 Hurricanes left Croydon 0950 hours, Personnel F/O. Bowring, P/O. Walker D.F.C. P/O. Simpson, P/O. Ritchie, Sgts Brown, Ekins and Sellars, P/O Atkinson, and were ordered to a position 6 miles north of Biggin Hill where a formation of 60 enemy bombers with their similar number of escort fights was attacked. Enemy bombers were in two blocks of 24 aircraft each flying level three abreast with 1 section of 3 aircraft flying in vic formation on each side, their height 16,000'. They were flying West towards Biggin Hill, but the whole formation swept south east when attacked.	
			Fighter escort was about 60 aircraft flying all around and above to a height of 25,000. F/O. Bowring flying Red 1 led the attack and was followed by the remainder of his section. Blue section did not engage, as Blue 1 had to dive down owing to oxygen trouble and was followed by the rest of Blue, and green sections. Red 1 had his machine damaged on the wings and fuselage by machine gun and canon shells, but after diving out of control from 15,000' to 1500' he chased an ME 109 out to sea and destroyed it to 10 miles S.S.W. of Dungeness. He twice caught up with ME 109 and beckoned the pilot to land, as he was obviously in a bad way, but each time the enemy pilot shook his fist, throttled back and opened fire. F/O. Bowring had previously destroyed one ME 109	

			probable and damaged a Dornier bomber. Red 3 Sgt Ekins destroyed one ME 109 probable which was seem to be diving out of control east of Dungeness. P/O. Ritchie and Sgt Silk who force landed at Lullington Castle with wound in his forearm, engaged but were unable to see result of their fire. Enemy Losses, 1 ME 109 destroyed. 2 ME 109 probable. 1 Do 17 damaged, Our Losses:- 1 Pilot wounded and machine damaged.	
Croydon.	6/9/40		Five Hurricanes 111 Squadron, were ordered to patrol base 0844 hours at 15,000. Red 1 F/O. Bowring experienced difficulty in hearing Runic, although he could hear Blue 1 clearly. He ordered Blue 1 to lead, but found he was too far astern, so he carried on, and led his section of 2 aircraft in a head-on attack on 40 Ju 88 as approaching Kenley from the directioned Maidstone, at 15,000'. F/O Bowring dived head-on from height of 18,000', followed by Red 2 Sgt Tweed. In the initial dive, result of their fire was not observed, but 1 Ju 98 which had come detached was shot down with both engines on fire by F/O. Bowring, and crashed between Kenley and Biggin Hill. F/O. Bowring had to land owing to a bullet smashing his windscreen, and Red 2 Sgt Tweed was shot down and crash landed, the pilot was injured. Blue section was flying astern and climbed to 20,000' where 10 ME 110 were engaged individually. 1 was claimed damaged by P/O. Simpson, flying Blue 1. Enemy losses:- 1 Ju 98 destroyed F/O. Bowring, 1 Me damaged P/O. Simpson. Our loss:- 1 Hurricane, Sgt Tweed injured. Personnel engaged were F/O. Bowring, P/O. Simpson, Sgts Wallace Tweed Hampshire. At 1730 hours squadron 9 Hurricanes were further engaged, on this occasion S/Ldr Thompson D.F.C. F/O. Bowring, P/O. Simpson, P/O. Ritchie, P/O Atkinson, Sgts Wallace, Brown Ekins Hampshire took part and were ordered to patrol Maidstone 20,000' and from there proceeded Thames Haven 20,000' and were ordered to intercept approaching formation of enemy bombers. Enemy bombers were seen by Sgt Hampshire flying at 12,000', but owing to haze and smoke from burning fires were not noticed by remainder of Squadron. He attempted to inform leader, but was unable to attract his attention, and consequently the raiders were not intercepted. Unfortunately 3 Heinkel 113 flying about 2,000' above the squadron dived very fast on	

		our leading sections and shot down F/O. Bowring who landed near Dartford, slightly wounded in the arm. Blue leader saw them dive and attempted to divert them by sending a burst from long range, but was unsuccessful. The ME 113 were coloured silver all over with black crosses under the wings. 8 Hurricanes landed between 1820 and 1845 hours.	
	7/9/40	S/Ldr Thompson, D.F.C. P/O. Walker D.F.C. P/O. Simpson, P/O. Atkinson, P/O. Ritchie, Sgts Brown, Ekins, Wallace and Hampshire were ordered to patrol Maidstone 20,000, at 1848 hours. Their height was then changed to 10,000' and then back to 20,000', this was unfortunate as the bombers formations were flying at about 15,000', and by the time they had regained the necessary height they were not in a favourable position to attack three large formations of enemy bombers passed over base and headed north east towards London. The escort of ME 110s circled the Aerodrome and awaited their return. One formation passed back over Croydon, the remainder evidently returned on a more easterly course. One section of a 111 intercepted enemy over base after they had reformed, and S/Ldr Thompson, D.F.C. Red 1 made a head-on attack on ME 110 Jaguars, these however changed course and a beam attack was delivered, Red leader spread the leading enemy section with a 4 sec burst, and Red 2 Sgt Ekins got in 2 bursts of 3 secs each. Blue 3 Sgt Brown also followed in with a 4 sec burst, the remainder of the squadron however, did not fire at all, or only got in small individual snap bursts, except Sgt Wallace, who had previously come down to re-fuel and took off again, he joined up with another Hurricane Squadron, and chased enemy bombers well out to sea, but his aircraft was damaged by an ME 109, and he had to glide back to shore as his engine was damaged. He baled out over Ashford at 1,000', and returned to base with slight injuries to his legs and head.	
	8/9/40	Squadron posted to Drem to reform. The following table of squadron and individual successes against enemy aircraft may be of interest, with the exception of 6 destroyed at Wick, they were all destroyed from the commencement of the campaign in France on the 18th of May until the Squadron was moved out of the line on the 7th September 1940.	

Hawker 'Hurricane' planes from 111 Squadron based at Northolt, in flight, c.1940.

			Destroyed.	Probably destroyed.	Damaged.	
		S/Ldr. Thompson. D.F.C.	6	1	4	
		F/Lt. Powell. D.F.C.	5	–	2	
Killed in action	10/8/40	F/Lt. Conners D.F.C. & Bar	10½	1	6½	
"	16/8/40	F/Lt. Ferriss. D.F.C.	9	2	1	
"	4/9/40	P/O. Maccinski	–	–	–	
"	4/9/40	F/O. Bruce.	6	–	3	
"	10/9/40	F/O. Higgs.	1	–	1	
		P/O. Walker D.F.C.	6	–	1	
		P/O. Simpson.	3½	1	3	Plus 1½
Killed in action	11/8/40	P/O. Copeman.	1	–		destroyed, 1 damaged with 64 S
"	11/8/40	P/O. Wilson.	2	–	2	
"	19/5/40	P/O. Bury.	1	–	–	
"	2/9/40	Sgt. Dymond. D.F.M.	9½	1	5	
		Sgt. Craig. D.F.M.	4	4	7	
		Sgt. Carnall.	½	–		
		Sgt. Robinson.	2	–	–	
		Sgt. BROWN	2	–	5	
		P/O. McIntyre.	1	–	–	
		F/O. Hardman.	–	–	½	

Killed in action	15/9/40	F/O. Fisher B.	–	–	1	
		P/O. Fisher A.	–	–	1	
		Sgt. Newton.	1	–	1	
		Sgt. Wallace.	6	3	7	
		Sgt. Deacon.	1	–	–	
		S/Ldr. McNab	1	–	–	
		F/Lt. Giddings	3	–	–	3 probably destroyed with 615 Sqdn
		F/O. Bowring.	3	2	4	
		P/O. Ritchie.	–	–	1	
		Sgt. Hampshire.	–	1	–	
		Sgt. Ekins	–	1	1	
Killed in action	18/5/40	F/Lt. Darwood.				
,,	19/5/40	P/O. Moorwood.				
Killed on active service	19/6/40	Sgt. Pascoe				
Killed in action	11/8/40	P/O. McKenzie.				
,,	11/8/40	Sgt. Sim.				
		Squadron Generally	9	1	1	
		ENEMY CASUALTIES	94	18	59	

Place.	Date.	Time.	Summary of Events.	References to Appendices
Drem	12/9/40		P/O. VIKOUKAL Posted to 111 from 25 Squadron. Posted to 75 Squadron Debden, effect 24/9/40. P/O. KAY J.K. Posted to 111 effect 11/9/40. Sgt. KOPEOKY Posted to 111 effect 12/9/40. Sgt. HAMPSHIRE Posted to 269 effect 10/9/40. Sgt. SELLARS Posted to 46 Squadron effect 16/9/40. P/O. RITCHIE Posted to 72 Squadron Biggin Hill effect 10/9/40. Sgt. ROBINSON Posted non-effective Kenley effect 31/7/40. Sgt. TWEED Posted non-effective Kenley effect 6/9/40. Sgt. EKINS Posted 501 Squadron Kenley effect 21/9/40. P/O. ATKINSON Posted 213 Squadron Tangmere effect 19/9/40. Sgt. SMYTH Returned to 111 Squadron from attachment 6 O.T.U. effect 19/9/40.	
	24/9/40		Sgt. WAGHORN Returned to 111 Squadron from attachment 6 O.T.U. effect 19/9/40. F/O. KUSTRYZNSKI Posted to 111 Squadron from 6 O.T.U. effect 31/8/40. Posted to 507 Squadron Tangmere effect 13/9/40. Sgt. BUMSTEAD Posted from 17 Squadron effect 26/8/40 detached Kenley re-attached 14/9/40. P/O. MACCINSKI Posted to 111 from 6 O.T.U. effect 31/8/40. Sub/Lt WALSH Posted to 111 from No 18 and 142 Squadrons effect 22/9/40. Sub/Lt WORRAL Posted to 111 from No 18 and 142 Squadrons effect 22/9/40. Sub/Lt RICHARDS Posted to 111 from No 18 and 142 Squadrons effect 22/9/40. Mid. GILBERT Posted to 111 from No 15 and 142 Squadrons effect 22/9/40. Sgt. BROWN. Promoted Pilot Officer with seniority 25/4/40. P/O. STEGMAN Posted to 111 Squadron effect 10/9/40. P/O. POPLAWSKI Posted to 111 Squadron effect 10/9/40.	

18/9/40 to 24/9/40	Sgt. MALIEJOWSKI Posted to 111 Squadron effect 10/9/40. Sgt. PAGE Posted to 111 Squadron from 6 O.T.U. effect 31/8/40. Sgt. PORTER Posted to 111 Squadron from 6 O.T.U. effect 31/8/40. P/O. GRAHAM Posted Kenley non-effective effect 26/8/40. Sgt. SILK Posted Kenley non-effective. Sgt. DEACON Posted Kenley non-effective. Effect 16/8/40. P/O. FISHER A. Posted 8 F.T.S. effect 24/8/40. P/O. ATKINSON Posted to 111 Squadron from 600 Squadron effect 24/8/40. P/O. RITCHIE Posted to 111 Squadron from 600 Squadron effect 24/8/40. F/O. BOWRING Posted to 111 Squadron from 600 Squadron effect 24/8/40. F/O. GRAHAM Posted to 111 Squadron from 600 Squadron effect 24/8/40. Sgt. NEWTON Posted to Kinley non-effective effect 18/8/40. Sgt. CARNALL Posted to Kinley non-effective effect 18/8/40.	
	Squadron through losses in action rendering its operational strength far below par is being used at the moment for training purposes, with the idea of posting the pilots when trained to 11 Group Squadrons as and when required. A nucleus of experienced pilots are being retained in the squadron for training purposes, and operational flying duties in this sector are being undertaken with the squadron personned as at present constituted as they are considered operationally trained for fighting purposes in this group.	
25/9/40	Sgt. Kopecky posted to 233 Squadron at Kenley effect 25/9/40 Squadron have been since May 18th thirty four times in action with the enemy, and have made in addition 15 offensive patrols over France, during the period of the invasion of Beleguim and the capitulation of the French Army, and including two patrols as bomber escort over Calaís and Boulogne.	

	26/9/40		P/O. Stegman posted to 229 Squadron, Northolt P/O. Poplawski posted to 229 Squadron, Northolt F/O. Bruce promoted Flight Lieutenant with effect	
	28/9/40		P/O. Kay posted to 257 Squadron Debden. Sgt. Page posted to 257 Squadron Debden.	
	29/9/40		P/O. Hitchings B.A.H. posted to 111 Squadron from 5 O.T.U. Aston Down, effect P/O. Harris P.A. posted to 111 Squadron from 5 O.T.U. Aston Down, effect Sgts J.B. Courtis, K. Dawick, A.H. Gregory, C.W. McDougal, E.C. Croker, J. Bayly posted from 6 O.T.U. Sutton Bridge, effect 28/9/40.	
	30/9/40		P/O. Harris posted to 3 Squadron, Turnhouse. P/O. Hitchings posted to 3 Squadron, Turnhouse.	

Commanding Officer

Recording Officer

FCCR/463/40.   SECRET.

FORM 'F'
FIGHTER COMMAND COMBAT REPORT

From: H.Q. 12 Group.   To: H.Q. Fighter Command.

(A)	Sector Serial No.	J.1.
(B)	Serial No. of order detailing patrol	36
(C)	Date	9.9.40.
(D)	Squadron 242	
(E)	No. of e/a.	Two formations of sixty with protecting fighters.
(F)	Type of e/a.	DO.215 ME. 110 ME. 109.
(G)	Time attack was delivered	Approx. 1740 hours.
(H)	Place attack was delivered	S.W. suburbs of London.
(J)	Height of e/a.	22,000 feet.
(K)	Enemy casualties	3 Do. 215}
		4 Me. 109} Destroyed.
		3 Me. 110}
(L)	Our casualties	Aircraft 2
(M)	Personnel	1 missing.
(N)	(i) Searchlights	N/A.
	(ii) Anti-aircraft guns assistance	Not very much.

(P) Range at which fire was opened in each attack on enemy together with estimated length of bursts.

RED 1	used 2,400 rounds	No stoppages
RED 2	" 460 "	do.
RED 3	just before going into attack found his oil pressure dud and returned to Duxford.	
YELLOW 1	fired 720 rounds	No stoppages, found one bullet in a/c. no damage to Duxford.
	Used cine camera gun.	
YELLOW 2	used 1,130 rounds, but does not make any claims.	
YELLOW 3	Sgt. R. H. Lonsdale had to bale out and is uninjured.	

BLUE 1	used 1,640 rounds	No stoppages, carried cine camera gun. Control cable was hit.
BLUE 2	used 1,680 rounds	No stoppages.
BLUE 3	used 2,400 rounds	No stoppages.
GREEN 1	used 2,320 rounds	No stoppages.
GREEN 2	used 1,320 rounds	No stoppages.
GREEN 3	K. M. Solanders is missing.	

(R) GENERAL

Squadron 242 were ordered to patrol North Weald – Hornchurch at 20,000 feet. They climbed to 22,000 feet and patrolled. At about 1740 hours saw a large enemy formation coming in from S–N about 15 miles S.W. of 242 Squadron, at 22,000 feet. The squadron turned and climbed to get above.

Enemy were in two large rectangular formations, one of approx. 60, then a space of a quarter of a mile and another 60 with a 500 feet step-up between them.

S/Ldr. Bader ordered his Squadron to attack in loose sections in line astern and to try and break up formations. Immediately some Me. 109 attacked his Squadron and in turn he had to attack them. S/Ldr., Red 1, attacked the leader and saw him turning away with white smoke pouring from both wings and was told afterwards that the e/a. went down in flames. The e/a. was a Do.215. He attacked several other e/a. but could not see results.

A salvo of bombs was seen to drop from the bombers who were still in formation, but there were plenty of stragglers. It was obvious that bombing was indiscriminate.

Red 2, P/O. W. L. McKnight, followed in with his leader and was immediately attacked by Me. 109 but succeeded in getting behind e/a, giving one short burst and seeing e/a. burst into flames. He was again attacked by two more but got in between them opening fire and saw bit of e/a. break off and dive to ground. He was still being attacked and his left aileron was blown off. He broke off engagement and in doing so saw his second Me. 109 crash to ground.

Yellow 1, F/Lt. G. E. Ball, took his and another section into attack. He dived through the formation and made a frontal attack on the leading section. He saw no effect of his fire but saw a Me. 109 and managed to get on e/a's tail. He gave him a burst of about 5 seconds and saw e/a. blow up in the sky.

Blue 1, F/Lt. G. Powell-Sheddon, went in with Yellow Section and dived to attack leader of bomber Group. He overshot and did not open fire but went into steep turn, attacking this time the second leader. He opened fire at about 50 yards at port engine of e/a. and noticed bullets strike engine and wing. Looking back he saw e/a's part engine on fire. He then himself got out of control for a short time, his starboard aileron control cable having been shot through, but managed to return to base.

Blue 2, P/O. R. Bush, dived in with his section and found a Me. 109 attacking him. He evaded e/a, climbed and saw Me.110 which he attacked. He gave it two short bursts and e/a burst into flames.

Blue 3, P/O. F. Tamblyn, saw 5 Me.110's detach themselves from the e/a. formation, make a right hand circle and attack our fighters. He saw an Me. 110 on the tail of a Hurricane and attacked, giving it two short bursts. E/a straightened up and both engines caught fire. He then went to the far side of the formation and saw a Me.110 cross his path so gave it a burst. E/a caught fire and crashed in front of cricket club house where he saw another a/c burning.

Green 1, Sgt. G. Richardson saw Do.215 which attempted to evade by turning steeply to the right. He got in a burst of six seconds and saw smoke coming from e/a. starboard engine. He regained position, made another attack from astern and port engine started to smoke. After the third attack e/a burst into flames.

Green 2, P/O. J. B. Latta, went in to attack the bombers, but found he was being attacked by e/a, Me.109. He evaded and managed to get in a dead astern attack for 6–8 seconds on an Me.109 which burst into flames. He was then attacked receiving a bullet in his part aileron but dived steeply and found no one on his tail so returned to base.

Weather was hazy up to 9,000 feet and clear above that height. Reflector sights were used by the whole squadron and generally satisfactory.

242 Squadron took off from Duxford 1700 hours and 10 a/c. landed at Duxford between 1800 and 1830 hours.

Rec. 1958 hours, 10.9.40.
FC/S 17570/INT. 11.9.40.

(signed) G. MAYBAUM F/LT.
Sector Intelligence Officer
COLTISHALL.

Squadron Leader Douglas Bader's Flying Log, 7–19 September 1940

YEAR 1940		AIRCRAFT		PILOT, OR 1ST PILOT	2ND PILOT, PUPIL OR PASSENGER	DUTY (INCLUDING RESULTS AND REMARKS)
MONTH	DATE	Type	No.			
—	—	—	—	—	—	TOTALS BROUGHT FORWARD
September	7th	Hurricane.	E.	Self.	—	From Duxford.
	8th	Hurricane.	S.	Self.	—	To Duxford.
	—	Hurricane.	D.	Self.	—	From Duxford.
	9th	Hurricane.	S.	Self.	—	To Duxford with Squadron
	—	Hurricane.	S.	Self.	—	Weald ret.
*	—	Hurricane.	S.	Self.	—	Patrolled London & intercepted enemy. Shot down 1 Do 215
	—	Hurricane.	S.	Self.	—	From Duxford.
	10th	Hurricane.	X	Self.	—	To Hucknall & return.
	12th	Hurricane.	D.	Self.	—	To Duxford & return.
	13th	Hurricane.	D.	Self.	—	To Duxford & return.
	14th	Hurricane.	D.	Self.	—	Squadron to Duxford.

SINGLE-ENGINE AIRCRAFT				PASS-ENGER	INSTR/CLOUD FLYING [Incl. in cols. (1) to (13)]	
DAY		NIGHT				
DUAL	PILOT	DUAL	PILOT		DUAL	PILOT
75.45	84.15	1.20	20.10		1.20	17.00
	.35					
	.30					
	.40					Patrolled London with Wing – 242, 310, 19. (242 leading).
	.30					Intercepted E/A Bombers and Fighters South of
	.20					Thames. Wing destroyed
	1.30				9/9/40	20 E/A. 242 Squadron got 11. I got the leader – a Do 215 in flames.
						P/O Sclanders killed
	.30					Sgt. Lonsdale baled out OK
	1.10					2 Hurricanes of 310 collided – 1 pilot OK. Baled out.
	1.00					
	1.00					
	.30				14/9/40	Awarded D.S.O. F/Lt Ball awarded D.F.C.

YEAR 1940		AIRCRAFT		PILOT, OR 1ST PILOT	2ND PILOT, PUPIL OR PASSENGER	DUTY (INCLUDING RESULTS AND REMARKS)
MONTH	DATE	Type	No.			
		Hurricane.	D.	Self.		Patrolled London area.
	—	Hurricane.	D.	Self.	—	Patrolled London & returned
*	15th	Hurricane.	D.	Self.	—	Patrolled London with wing. Shot down one Do.17.
	—	Hurricane.	D.	Self.	—	Offensive, wing patrol
	—	Hurricane.	D.	Self.	—	Return to Coltishall
	16th	Hurricane.	D.	Self.	—	To Duxford & patrol N. Weald
	—	Hurricane.	D.	Self.	—	To Coltishall from Duxford.
	17th	Hurricane.	D.	Self.	—	To Duxford.
	—	Hurricane.	D.	Self.	—	London patrol.
	—	Hurricane.	D.	Self.	—	To Coltishall.
	18th	Hurricane.	D.	Self.	—	To Duxford.

GRAND TOTAL TOTALS CARRIED   FORWARD   930 Hrs 55 Mins

SINGLE-ENGINE AIRCRAFT				PASS-ENGER	INSTR/CLOUD FLYING [Incl. in cols. (1) to (13)]	
DAY		NIGHT				
DUAL	PILOT	DUAL	PILOT		DUAL	PILOT
	1.30					1) Wing patrolled London. Engaged enemy formation & destroyed most of them. Wing comprised 242, 310, 302, 19 and 611. Eric Ball shot down – OK.
	2.00					
	1.30					
	.50					2) Sighted large enemy formation & tried to attack, but too low. Was attacked by ME 109s & had to break away. Spun off Xxxxxx Xxxxxx's* slipstream & out of the fight. <u>Wing total for day: 52 + 8</u>.
	.30					
	1.30					
	.30					Georgie P S shot down baled out. <u>242 Total: 12</u>
	.30					
	1.25					
	.20					
	.30					
75.45	833.35	1.20	20.10		1.20	17.00

* Bader seems to make reference to a pilot whose name is partly illegible and does not match those in 242 Squadron. It seems that he did, however, find himself in P/O Denis Crowley-Milling's slipstream before going into a spin.

A pilot of 6 Squadron RAF stands by his Hawker Hurricane Mark IID at Shandur, Egypt. This view shows the 40mm Vickers anti-tank cannon fitted to the Mark IID, which the squadron employed to good effect in the fighting in North Africa.

T.C. 32

SECRET
HURRICANE IID AIRCRAFT
(ANTI-TANK ROLE)
REPORT ON OPERATIONS OF NO. 6 SQUADRON R.A.F.
(MIDDLE EAST) JUNE/NOVEMBER 1942

FOREWORD

This report is reproduced verbatim and circulated as a T.C. paper for the information of all concerned. It amplifies the earlier reports embodied in T.C. 27, which can now be regarded as obsolete, and embodies both tactical, technical and training information.

I. <u>INTRODUCTION</u>

1. This report covers the period when No. 6 Squadron, R.A.F., in the role of an anti-tank Squadron, commenced operating in the Western Desert in June, 1942, just prior to the withdrawal, the static period on the Alamein Line, and later, the start of the 8th Army Advance.

2. The Squadron was trained at Shandur, Egypt, for about five weeks, mainly in May. Training was very much held up in the early stages by the lack of aircraft and equipment, and at the beginning of June, although far from having completed its training, two flights of the Squadron with 9 aircraft proceeded to the Western Desert. One remained at Shandur to carry on training as best they could with at first two, later one, aircraft. In the desert, the pilots' shooting rapidly appeared to improve, although it was a considerable time before they could fire more than three pairs per run, also concentrate on firing the "S" guns and fire the Brownings at the same time. The increased use of the latter has since increased considerably the number of tanks and lorries which have been set on fire.

3. The original 16 pilots in the Squadron were all Army Co-operation trained and all fairly experienced. This was found to be invaluable, as a very high standard of map reading, identification and a close study of ground forces is essential.

II. <u>TACTICS LEADING TO ATTACK</u>

4. During the early stages of operations the Hurricane IID's operated in flights of three aircraft flying in line astern, with one squadron of Kittybombers, one aircraft leading and the remainder on either side, as close cover, and one squadron of Kittybombers as top cover. This was adopted as the Kittybombers were very familiar with that part of the country. The formation went out at about 5 to 6,000 feet until over the target, the Kittybombers dived down and released their bombs at the same time the Flight or Flights of Hurricane IID's broke away and dived down to about 1,000 yards from the target, where they flattened out at about 15 feet from the ground and made their attack.

5. Very heavy A/A was encountered in these attacks. Great difficulty was experienced in picking out tanks from the various M.T. on the dive down and attack, and quite impossible on the approach to the target area, at the height the Kittybombers used to fly in order to avoid the

A/A fire. In a number of cases tanks which were thought to be there were not found. The Hurricane IID's had to fly at +1 lb. per sq. inch boost in order to keep up with the Kittybombers. It took the Army Co-operation trained pilots a very short time before they knew the country as well as the fighter pilots, also their own pin-pointing was much more accurate. From that time onwards the Hurricane IID's led all the formations, going out at 180 m.p.h. indicated 2400 R.P.M. 0 boost, with one squadron of Kittyhawks weaving as close cover and one squadron as top cover. This put the range of the IID up from about 75 miles to 95 miles radius of action allowing enough petrol for three attacks and about 15 minutes searching over the target area.

6. Later, it was decided that a good target for Anti-tank Squadrons was not a good target for the Fighter-bombers, so two squadrons of cover were provided, without the bomber diversion as used at first. During this period, the withdrawal from Bir Hacheim to Alamein, there were numbers of excellent targets and a large number of Anti-tank aircraft could have been used to great advantage.

7. A number of successful anti-tank sweeps were carried out by No. 6 Squadron, with medium cover and high cover, in the southern sector of the Alamein line. The country was fairly open desert with the normal small wadis and sand dunes etc., here and there were quite a lot of armoured patrols operating, which could be attacked without large numbers of M.T. in the vicinity. The latter were always avoided where possible, as the German M.T. appears to carry a very large amount of very effective light A/A. On these sweeps the Hurricane IID used to search an area for about 15 minutes, attacking any armour that they saw.

8. When working with the Kittybomber, the operations of the Squadron were controlled by a Wing Headquarters. Subsequently No.6 Squadron was [illegible] for its own operations and choice of targets, rarely asking No. 211 Group for fighter cover, which was always produced.

9. The most usual number of IID's employed has been either 3 or 6 aircraft, according to the target. These are escorted out and home by a squadron of medium and high cover. This escort is essential, since in no way can the IID be considered as a normal fighter, the extra weight carried and the harmonisation of the guns alone precluding this. In

order to keep changing the formations, 4 or 6 aircraft sometimes work in pairs, which looks rather like an ordinary fighter formation giving cover.

10. The formation usually adopted has been, in the case of six aircraft, two loose Vics in line astern, and in the case of three aircraft, one loose Vic. Each member of the formation keeps a good look out for enemy aircraft. It is not, however, possible, to keep such a sharp lookout as would be the case in a normal fighter, since the greatest attention must be paid to map reading, in order to find the target and to fly out along the selected route. Map reading plays a very important part, as it is essential to know exactly where one is for fear of attacking our own troops. Also by following the routes given in briefing, a large amount of A/A fire can be avoided.

11. The formation goes out at a height of 3,000 feet, which is considered to be above the effective range of small arms fire, and below the level of [illegible] bursts. Speed is maintained at 180 m.p.h. until the target area is approached, where it is increased to 200 m.p.h. On approaching the target, height is lost to 1,500 feet since at this height observation of ground objects is considerably more accurate. At the same time each Vic changes into line astern.

III. <u>THE ATTACK</u>

12. On sighting the target the formation goes down to a height of 15/20 feet and approximately 1,000 yards away. On the leader turning into the target, the formation turns inside him and goes into the attack in a rough echelon, each member of the formation selecting his own target. The approach is made at a speed of 240 m.p.h., since the datum line is then 2° down, sights being set parallel. Variations of more that 30 m.p.h. will affect the accuracy of the shooting. Fire is opened at 700 yards closing to 2,000 yards, and both Brownings and "S" Guns are used. The Brownings and "S" guns are harmonised at 500 yards. After each burst of one shell per gun the sights are realigned on the target. Normally about 5 bursts can be got in on each attack. The breakaway is made before reaching the target if possible, to avoid being hit by splinters and the area is cleared by low flying weaving.

13. If the tanks are isolated, up to three attacks can be made. This is left to the Flight Commander, and depends on A/A fire encountered.

Breakaways were always made towards our own line – this may have been the cause of only one pilot missing during operations.

14. During this time, the escort remains above ready to escort the IID's home. If, however, they lose sight of the IID's, they should remain in the area sufficiently long to draw any possible opposition away from them. The IID's, when away from the danger area, climb up to meet their cover at a point previously fixed as a rendezvous, but in the event of being separated, they fly home at nought feet. The escort is told before take-off how long the IID's will remain in the target area.

15. All the Flight Leaders were Army Co-operation trained. At the time of writing the fighter trained pilots had not sufficient desert experience to be Flight Leaders.

16. As far as possible wireless silence is maintained until on the homeward journey.

IV. <u>CASUALTIES</u>

17. On all operations from June to November, casualties from No. 6
Squadron have amounted to one pilot and aircraft missing.

> 10 Aircraft Category I.
>
> 9 Aircraft Category II.
>
> 6 Aircraft Category III.

of which 4 aircraft were left in enemy hands, it being impossible to
salvage them in time. All pilots with the exception of one either walked
to or were picked up by our own troops.

18. The casualties in No. 7 Squadron were

> 1 Aircraft Category III.
>
> 2 Aircraft Category I.

19. The total number of sorties carried out were

> No. 6 Squadron – 162
>
> No. 7 Squadron – 18

V. <u>TARGETS ENGAGED</u>

20. The first few targets consisted of a comparatively small number of tanks
well dispersed among about 600 M.T. The Kittybombers were used
to bomb the transport to act as a diversion for the A/A fire. On every
occasion very heavy A/A fire was encountered, resulting in about 4 out
of every 6 Hurricane IID's being Cat. II (beyond Unit repair).

21. As the Germans advanced, a number of perfect targets were found
consisting of a number of tanks which were about to attack our troops,
and had proceeded ahead of their supporting transport. On none of
these targets was any opposition encountered from the ground, except
a little small arms fire.

22. When the situation became static, it was once again found that no
opposition was made by tanks on their own, but on every occasion the
supporting M.T. was extremely well equipped with light A/A guns. On
examination of captured German and Italian tanks, it was seen that the
anti-aircraft armament was very bad and difficult to use.

23. The best time for an anti-tank squadron to attack tanks is when they are
about to attack or be attacked from the ground. At this time, all their
guns are lowered, the tanks closed, and the crews are not able to see or
hear aircraft, also at such a time the soft skinned transport with the flak
must be left behind. These targets appear frequently but in most cases

it was found that by the time information had been received by No. 6 Squadron and fighter cover arranged, the target had moved and was not worth attacking. During the static period, various methods were tried out with the object of reducing this time lag.

VI. INFORMATION AND COMMUNICATION

24. Great difficulties have been experienced in getting information of targets back quickly enough for action to be taken on it. Reports from Air sources were much too slow and on the whole most inaccurate. It is essential that the minimum amount of time is allowed to lapse between the reporting and the dispatch of the Hurricane IID's.

25. At first all information regarding targets was obtained from Air sources, i.e. Fighters, Fighter-bombers and T/R. Directly the situation started to become static, the anti-aircraft fire encountered by the Fighter and Fighter-bombers was increased, causing them to fly over the target areas rather higher, as a result they were unable to see the tanks, also the few targets they did see had to be verified before No. 6 Squadron was allowed to attack. This meant large delays, resulting in a number of abortive sorties, as the target had usually moved by the time the Hurricane IID's arrived. The same applied to the T/R information. It was then found that the most accurate and quickest information was received from ground sources.

VII. TARGET REPORTING

26. Reports of targets have been received from various sources such as Tac/R, Kittybombers and patrolling armoured cars. At present, reports from forward armoured cars are being frequently used. These patrols are equipped with R/T, and transmit information back to Regimental H.Q. which passes the information on to Brigade H.Q. at which there is situated an A.S.C. tentacle. The tentacle then transmits the message on the normal A.S.C. network back to Air Support Control, which is situated at present at Combined Army/Air Headquarters. The O.C. A.S.C. is instructed to filter all messages received from tentacles with a special view to identifying targets suitable for the IID's. When the A.O.C. or his representative at Army/Air Headquarters agrees that the IID's should answer a request received from a tentacle, the order to attack is sent over the normal rear links of the A.S.C. Unit.

27. Considerable time has been saved by installing a wireless set at Army/ Air Headquarters which maintains a listening watch to intercept on the Divisional net. An Army Liaison officer from the Armoured Division Headquarters was located at the A.S.C. at Army/Air Headquarters and can advise the commanders on the suitability of targets received from the Armoured Division Headquarters. The order to attack and relevant information is then passed from Army/Air Headquarters to the squadron on a rear 'one to one' W/T link. This link was also used to pass a large amount of information of movements in the target area, also information available at Air Support Control for use in the briefing.

VIII. BRIEFING

28. All briefing and interrogation of pilots was done by the A.L.O's. A most detailed situation map was kept up. From this map it was possible to brief pilots as to the best direction of attack, the lie of the land, A/A positions, areas in which M.T. was to be found. If hit by A/A, what areas were the most suitable to force land in. Also what the pilots were likely to see of our own troops and armour.

29. Points which are always brought out at the briefing are as follows:-
    (i)   Nature of Operation.
    (ii)   Description of Target and Pin Point.
    (iii)   Enemy Forces.
    (iv)   Our Forces.
    (v)   Leaders of Formations and Sub-formations.
    (vi)   Tactics over target.
    (vii)   Time allowed over target.
    (viii) Escort and R.V.
    (ix)   Course out and time – landmarks.
    (x)   Way home – L.G's – action if alone.
    (xi)   Rations – chits.
    (xii)   Petrol Check.
    (xiii) Wireless Silence and which button to be used.

30. Numerous visits were made by the A.L.O's and members of the squadron to the forward troops to explain the reason for the information required, and how the pilots could be assisted in locating their target quickly by firing smoke at a given E.T.A., firing very lights, displaying

ground strips or coloured smoke if available. These methods met with varying success.

31. Before each operation pilots were issued with emergency rations to be carried in their pockets, Italian money and various aids in case they had to walk home.

32. It is considered that two A.L.O's and a small section are sufficient for each anti-tank Squadron on any operations.

33. Information received by interrogation was considerable. Most of the pilots, being fairly experienced in Army Co-operation work, automatically used to carry out a search of the area over which they flew. This was passed immediately to the Air Support Controls.

IX. READINESS

34. Six aircraft were kept at 30 minutes notice on the downwind side of the aerodrome. It was found that the Hurricane IID aircraft could be off in a lot less than 30 minutes, but by the time arrangements had been made for fighter cover and they had reached their rendezvous over the Anti-tank Squadron Aerodrome, the 30 minutes was up.

35. Sorties were never sent out with the object of ground-straffing lorries, etc. Sometimes attacks were made on lorries in mistake for tanks. If, having completed an attack on a tank and on break away, lorries were seen in their sights, pilots were told to have a quick shot at them with both .303 Brownings and "S" Guns. This resulted in the large assortment of vehicles on which direct hits were claimed. Explosive ammunition would be more suitable for lorries.

X. GENERAL

(i) G.45 Cine Camera Gun

36. Very little benefit has been gained from the G.45 Cine Guns either in training or in operations. It was found that the lag units installed in the aircraft to enable the camera gun to continue running after single shots had been fired, was too slow and in nearly every case only about six frames were taken of the target, then, a considerable amount of sky was photographed after the aircraft

had broken away. The cameras were then tried wired direct to the master switch, but in a lot of cases the pilot, in the excitement of operations, forgot to switch on. Some bedside electric light switches of the push bell type were then tried in place of the normal camera gun press button on the stick. The pilot has only to move his thumb and press the button and the camera continues running until the button is pressed a second time. This has been found quite successful. The pilot can hear the camera turning on the R/T, so can tell if switch is on or not. The master switch retains its normal function.

37. The actual films have not been very clear and a negative film shown on a screen does not give a very good idea where the shots are going. In the desert if a shot falls short, the target is covered with dust and it is quite impossible to see what is being attacked in the Cine Camera Gun film.

(ii) R/T

38. For the first three months the Squadron was fitted with TR9D. HF. Radio sets. It was thought that there was some fault with the bonding of Hurricane IID aircraft, as background interference from Air to Air made R/T practically impossible to use. The quality of the R/T on the ground without the engine running was perfect. As soon as the engine was started, the quality went down about 30% and when the engine was run up it went down to about 60%. The reason for this interference was never traced.

39. In August sufficient V.H.F. sets had been made available for all the aircraft in the Squadron to be fitted. Since the change over to V.H.F. the R/T has been quite satisfactory both air to air and ground to air or vice versa, although the range of the latter is very limited by low flying.

(iii) Equipment

40. Aircraft at all times carried full desert rations, 2¾ gallons of water and various means of signaling in case of forced landings. At all times on the ground, covers were kept on the "S" Guns, which were removed when the pilot was ready to take off. Also covers were always kept on the pilot tube, radiators, air intakes, cockpit

and engine covers over the exhausts. Metal covers which could be clipped on to the radiator and air intakes were made so not to waste any time taking them off.

<u>Prepared by No. 6 Squadron (Middle East)</u>
<u>January 1943.</u>
<u>Reproduced and circulated by Air Ministry (D.A.T.)</u>
<u>March 1943.</u>
<u>S. 9092.</u>

Index